MORE BETTER HAPPY

How To Get More of What You Want,
Have a Better Life,
and Be Happy

Mark Coté

MORE BETTER HAPPY

Published by Mark Coté
Paperback ISBN: 978-0-9987303-0-1
Cover Design: Mark Coté
Copyright © cover images BigstockPhoto.com
Copyright © 2017 Mark Coté.

Dedication

To Mom, Memeré Cote, Debbie, Terry, Nancy, Kirsten, Sarah, Danielle, Michele, Lisa, Maggie and Aubrey. You are the women who shaped, guided, inspired and supported me in becoming the person I am today. Thank you.

Introduction

I was discussing the concept of getting more of what you want, having a better life and being happy with someone and they said to me:

"It's easy for you, you're a naturally happy person."

"Ha ha ha ha ha ha ha ha ha ha!"

I thought that was the funniest thing I ever heard. Me, naturally happy? Nope, that's not me.

I grew up in an alcoholic household. I am the son of an alcoholic. I'm also the nephew and cousin of a few alcoholics. Oh yeah, and I'm an alcoholic. My addiction didn't limit itself to alcohol, it embraced drugs and cigarettes as well. My life, both growing up and as a grown up, is full of experiences that are anything but happy.

I've also gotten divorced after eighteen years of marriage, declared bankruptcy after getting myself into six figure credit card debt, been unable to pay rent and had a place to live only through the benevolence of a family member.

I wake up most mornings feeling crappy and thinking crappy thoughts. I am not a naturally happy person.

Those experiences, thoughts and feelings do not define who I am. I decide who I am going to be and what I am going to do and have. I learned that from Zig Ziglar, and I consider that to be the essence of personal development.

"Wait a minute, Mark, I'm not into that personal development stuff."

Really? Why not? You should be. This book is about getting more of what you want, having a better life and being happy. That implies that you are unhappy with your life, at least in some areas, because you're not getting enough of what you want, which would result in a better life. How are you going to do that?

It would be great if human beings came with an instruction manual. And not those crappy IKEA instructions with drawings that are hard to decipher and no words. After all, most human beings are way more complicated than a piece of IKEA furniture. But, unfortunately, we don't. With no clear cut directions or instructions, most of us muddle through life, doing the best we can, dissatisfied, unfulfilled and unhappy, to various degrees.

Malcolm Gladwell, in his book "The Outliers", attributes becoming successful or achieving mastery in any field as a result of practicing or working in your field for ten thousand hours. It's not enough to just show up, you must study and practice and work at it if you want to get better at something.

How much study, practice and work have you done to learn how to get more of what you want, have a better life and be happy? For most people, the answer is none. Typically, it's not taught at home or in church. It's not a subject that is taught in school. You can't get an undergraduate or graduate degree in it. Nowhere in the traditional educational system are you taught about your unlimited potential and how to tap into that to create the life you desire.

That's why people choose to study personal development. That's why I started studying personal development forty years ago. I choose to work on being happy every day of my life. I replace the crappy thoughts with happy thoughts, and then I feel happy. By the time I start interacting with other people I am a happy person. Because every morning I chose to be happy and do what it takes to be happy.

You may perceive personal development as a big deal, or something that's hard to do. It's not. In fact, you've been doing it all your life. Are you the same person you were at five years old, or fifteen, or twenty-five? At five years old you were focused on playing, learning to ride a bike and being excited about starting school. At fifteen your focus was on getting your driver's license, your popularity in high school and your burgeoning sexual awareness. At twenty-five your focus had shifted to your career, romantic relationships and starting a family.

Whether or not those were the specific things you were focused on, your focus was different during each of those decades because you were different. As you progress through life, the things you learn and experience cause you to grow and change. It happens organically, without any direct input or control by you. Personal development is the process of using focus and intention to become the person that does what it takes to have what you desire.

Getting what you want, having a better life and being happy are results. This book will show you how you can get the results you desire while looking at life as a game. So not only will you create the life you desire for yourself, you'll have fun doing it.

Enough talking about it, turn the page and let's get started.

Chapter One

You Are Amazing!

You are Amazing! Awesome! Incredible!

Do you see it? Feel it? Know it to the core of your being? You used to. In fact, you were born knowing and believing it.

About nine months before you were born, you went up against 200 million others in a race. It was the most important race of your existence. It was, literally, a race for life. It was the Race to the Egg. And you won!

That's right, out of all of those swimmers, only a few hundred overcome all the obstacles that stood between them and the egg, and you were one of them. Incredibly, you had overcome almost 200 million others. Once you got there, you and the other survivors worked relentlessly to breach the barrier that surrounded and protected the egg. With single minded focus and determination, **you** were the one to break the final barrier and fertilize the egg.

Whoo hoo, go you! Right from the start you were an action hero. If any other sperm had beaten those odds and won that race you wouldn't be you, you'd be someone else. That was an amazing success, it was totally awesome, an incredible feat.

This is who You are, the Real and Authentic You. The Real You is a being of unlimited potential and limitless possibilities. The Real You is connected to the Universe and knows how to create whatever You desire. The Real You does not judge, manipulate, or seek to have power and control over others. The Real You is loving and accepting and happy. This is who You were when You were born. The Real and Authentic You still lives within you.

Your potential may not have been apparent when you first entered the world. You had a tiny body, a scrunched-up face and you cried as you took your first breaths in what seemed like a harsh and alien environment after the comfort of the womb. However, it's not what's on the outside that determines what you can do. As my yoga instructor says, it's an inside job. Humble beginnings are no indication of your destination. It's a tiny acorn that grows into a mighty oak tree. Like the acorn, you were designed to do great things and fulfill your destiny.

When you were born, about all you could do was eat, sleep, poop and cry. Those limitations did not last long. The desire to do, accomplish, understand and succeed is hard wired into you. You knew this when you were born and you were relentless in your pursuit of those goals. Any parent of a small child can tell you how the child's energy and enthusiasm to explore and learn can exhaust them by the end of the day.

The Power To Create

You were born with the power to create. You do it all the time. It is one of the most powerful forces in the Universe and it exists within you. You can use that power to create anything you desire. Wow, that's pretty awesome, right? So where does this amazing power come from?

Your ability to create stems from the only thing in the Universe you have direct control over. You know you don't have control over other people. I'm sure there are times you've tried to control someone else like a parent, child, spouse, boss, employee or co-worker. I'll bet it didn't turn out the way you wanted. You also know you can't control the weather or traffic. At this point in your life that should be painfully obvious.

So the obvious answer is you. You are the only thing you have direct control over. Let's get more specific. What is one thing is under your direct control and is also the source of your ability to create anything you desire?

It's your thoughts! The only thing in the Universe over which you have direct control is your thoughts.

Boom goes the dynamite! Do you realize how incredibly awesome this is? The only thing you control is your thoughts and by controlling your thoughts you can create anything you truly desire. That's amazing!

Everything you have in your life was created by your thoughts. Everything you desire starts first as a thought. Your thoughts create the emotions and actions that generate the results in your life. It's a simple cause and effect relationship. Your thoughts are the cause that generate your emotions and direct your actions which then create the results, or the effect.

When you were young you saw everyone else walking and you thought you would do that too. That thought created a burning desire to walk. It was a process. First you learned to pull yourself up to standing. Then you took a step or two while holding on to something to support yourself. Finally, you let go and, holding your arms out to balance yourself, you toddled for a step or two before you fell down. Undaunted, you got back up and tried it again. And again, and again, and again until, finally, you were walking. No one did that for you, no one can do that for you. Your thoughts, emotions and actions created the result and ever since that day you can walk.

You don't just have the power to create the results in your life, you can create things that don't exist until you think of them. If you can think of it, you can create it. Everything that humankind has created started out first as a thought. That thought was energized and empowered through emotions and action and manifested into existence.

Our ancestors saw lightning create a fire. They liked the fire, it could be used to warm them and cook food and provide light in the darkness. Someone had the thought to find a way to create fire on demand. And they did.

Planes, trains and automobiles; radio and television; computers and smart phones; at one point in time they didn't exist. They all started out as an idea, a thought that ultimately resulted in the manifestation of the physical item.

The creation process requires the use of both your conscious and subconscious mind. Creation starts with a thought in the conscious mind. As your conscious mind focuses on the thought it creates an emotion, like desire. That emotion energized thought is passed on to the subconscious. Once that happens, the subconscious will then work to manifest that which the conscious mind requested.

As I mentioned, it all starts with a conscious thought. Not only do you have this amazing power, but it's the only thing in the Universe you have direct control over. If you're not sure you control your thoughts, think of an elephant or the Eiffel Tower or your mother's face. Think of anything you want, just put a picture in your head. See? If you can choose to think of something, and put a picture of it in your head, then you have direct control over your thoughts.

Of course, just because you **can** control your thoughts, doesn't mean that you **do** control your thoughts.

I purposely use the term direct control because your thoughts have indirect control over two other things - your emotions and your actions. Again, this is easily verified. Try to have an emotion without having a thought first. You can't do it. If you want to feel angry you must first think of something that makes you angry. Same with happy, scared, frustrated and any other emotion. Whatever emotion you are experiencing right now, try and feel something different without having a thought first. You can't, because your emotions are a result of your thoughts.

The same is true when it comes to taking action. Before you can do anything you must first think about doing it. What about when you see something coming at you out of the corner of your eye and you have no time to think but you still dodge or duck or deflect to avoid it? In that case, it's your subconscious mind generating the thought, because it can react much quicker than your conscious mind. Regardless of which mind it was, conscious or subconscious, there was a thought that preceded your action.

Your Amazing Mind

Your thoughts, the force behind your power to create all that you desire, reside in your conscious and subconscious mind. Let's take a brief look at how your mind operates.

The primary job of your conscious mind is to analyze all the information from your senses, to understand what it means and what, if anything, you should do. That's a really big job considering your senses can bombard you with up to two million bits of information. That's a lot of data to process. It's especially challenging since your conscious mind can only process about seven bits of sensory information at one time.

Your conscious mind's job is made even more difficult by the fact that it can only focus on one thing at a time. You might be wondering "But what about multitasking?" Sorry, your mind does not multitask. Your conscious mind can switch between areas of focus very rapidly, giving the appearance of focusing on more thing at once, or multitasking. I used to be really good at that when I was younger. Today, not so much. If you talk to me while I'm focused on doing something else I'm probably not going to hear a word you say.

The bottom line is that, if you had to consciously process all the data you received from your senses, you would be overwhelmed to the point of immobility.

What's a conscious mind to do? It calls upon its talented and powerful partner, the subconscious mind. While your conscious mind is focused in its limited way, the subconscious is working behind the scenes like some super computer. It has a few tricks up its sleeve to help out your conscious mind.

Your subconscious realizes that there's a lot of sensory data that doesn't require any conscious processing. Things like the warmth of the sunshine, the breeze blowing across your skin, your heartbeat, the sounds of traffic, the smell of dinner cooking, the chair pressing against your back and thighs and so forth require no conscious processing. Unless you choose to focus on any of these things your subconscious says "Meh, who cares?" and filters them out, or deletes them, letting your conscious mind focus on whatever does require your attention in the moment.

Nice.

Another useful trick is the ability to do certain things, like tie a shoelace or ride a bike, without conscious thought. Repetition and practice causes these skills to be deeply embedded in your subconscious mind. This allows you to perform those tasks automatically, without conscious thought. This is why athletes work on the basic moves and skills of their sport, so that executing them becomes automatic. This is known as muscle memory, although the actual term is procedural memory. It can also be a bit scary. Have you ever driven somewhere and been so focused on something in your conscious mind that you have no recollection of driving there?

Nifty - and a bit disconcerting.

Your subconscious realizes it's very inefficient to process the same sensory information every time you encounter it. So your subconscious mind creates associations between thoughts, emotions and behaviors to facilitate the process. Let me give you an example of what I mean.

On your first birthday, your parents present you with your very first cupcake. At age one, you're not doing a lot of high end conscious thinking and reasoning. You wave your arms around a bit and grab the cupcake and smoosh it between your fingers. The people around you laugh which makes you feel good and encourages you. You like the squishy way it feels so you decide to go for some more sensory input and you stuff some of it in your mouth. As the cake and frosting dance over your taste buds, the pleasure centers in your brain go crazy from the sheer deliciousness of that sugary confection. You don't stop stuffing it into your face until it's gone and then you look around for more.

Your subconscious immediately creates an association between the sight and smell of cupcakes, eating them and feeling awesome. Now you don't have to consciously figure out cupcakes every time you encounter them. In the future, when you see a cupcake, you will associate pleasure and goodness with it and you are going to stuff that cupcake in your mouth as fast as you can, no thought required.

The opposite can happen as well. If you eat something that makes you sick, your subconscious might create a link between the food and feeling nauseous and you'll never touch that particular food item again.

Another way your subconscious helps your conscious mind is by creating beliefs. A belief is a thought or idea you accept as true regardless of proof. As a young child you saw a hot burner on the stove and wanted to touch it in order to gain more sensory information so you could figure out what it was and what you should do. Your parents knew that what you should do is leave it alone so they told you "Hot!" and "No!" and pulled your hand away so you wouldn't burn yourself. But your conscious mind didn't really understand why you shouldn't touch the burner, and it still wanted to touch the burner in order to figure it out. You managed to touch it and burnt your hand and immediately felt pain.

That was something you understood and your mind created an instant association around this painful experience, just like it did with the pleasurable experience of the cupcake. The next time your parents told you "No!" about touching something, you remembered the hot burner and what happened when you touched it. Instead of touching whatever it is, you decide not to touch it based on what your parents told you. You accepted what they told you as true without the proof of actually touching it. That's a belief.

You started creating associations and beliefs when you were born and you continue to create them today. You have associations and beliefs about everything, and I do mean literally everything. You have a ton of beliefs and associations about yourself; what you can and can't do, what you're good at and what you're not good at, whether you are pretty, handsome, talented, agile, clumsy, smart, dumb, friendly, athletic, etc. You have beliefs about your parents, children, siblings, boss, coworkers, spouse or significant other. You have them about the types of television shows, movies, music, and books you like and don't like. Every opinion or thought you have about anything probably is based on an association or belief.

The first time you encounter something your mind creates an association or belief about it. If you're not trying to figure out what something is or what it means, then you already have a belief or association about it. Associations and beliefs are not set in stone. They can change based on new experiences or sensory input. If you think about it, you can probably identify a lot of associations and beliefs you have today that have changed over the years.

That's You, the Real and Authentic You. A being of unlimited potential and limitless possibilities. You have the power to create anything you desire by utilizing the one thing in the Universe you have direct control over, your thoughts.

Chapter Two

Why Your Life Sucks

You might be wondering "Mark, what the heck? My life doesn't suck!"

Really? If what I told you in the last chapter is true, and I assure you, it is, then there is no reason for you not to have everything you desire. Do you have everything you desire? Probably not. That sucks!

When I say your life sucks, what I really mean is that it sucks that you don't have everything you desire. Do you see people who are what you want to be, do things you want to do, and have things you want to have? If you look around you, and pay attention, you'll see people creating what they want all over the place. Why them and not you?

Simple, they've figured out how to play the game. That's right, life is like a game and everything you want is a result that you are playing for. When you win, you get what you want. When you lose, you don't get what you want. Chances are good you have some of the things you desire, so you're winning some of the time. This book will help you understand the game, the rules, your opponent and how to win. Once you learn these things all you have to do is play the game, with awareness and a focus on getting better, so you win more often.

Why do I say that life is like a game? That's an analogy, a way of explaining something by comparing it to something else. I like the analogy of a game because games are fun, and who doesn't want to have fun? I also like the fact that when a game is over, it's not the end. I grew up playing pinball, and, after the final ball was lost, the words "Play Again" would light up. So when I lost a game, or didn't get the result I was playing for, I always had the chance to play again.

I invite you to view your life the same way, like a game. This book is like a cheat sheet, or hack, to help you win more often. As you play the game, and play for the results you want in your life, you're going to win some and lose some. No worries, remember, every time you lose a game you get to play again. The more you play, the better you'll get, and the more you'll win.The game of life is quite simple. You play for results, things you want to be, do and have. When you achieve the result you're playing for, you win. When you achieve a different result, you lose. If you lose, or achieve a different result than the one you were playing for, you get to play again. In fact, you can keep playing until you win, or get the result you desire. Simple, right?

Every game has rules, what you are and are not allowed to do in order to win. When playing the game of life, the biggest rule is to do no harm to others. All religious and philosophical teachings talk about existing in harmony with the world around us and treating others with love, kindness and respect. I don't think I need to spell that out for you. Unless you have a severe mental disorder, you know the difference between what we call right and wrong in the context of other people. So when playing the game of life the first rule is simple, do no harm.

The game of life is not a zero sum game. A zero sum-game is one in which one player's wins, or gains, are offset by another player's losses. When the gains and losses are added together the net result is zero. In other words, for you to win someone else has to lose and for another player to win you must lose. Life is not like that. Life is a game of abundance. There is more wealth today than ever before and more wealth is being created every day. Life is like an iTunes download. How many times can a file be downloaded from iTunes before it runs out and nobody else can download it? The answer is it never runs out, it can be downloaded again and again, forever and ever.

You're not playing the game of life against other people. It's not that kind of a game. You're playing for the results you desire, the things you want to be, do and have in your life. If you've ever been to an arcade, you may be familiar with Skee Ball. It's like a miniature bowling lane stuck on legs and set on an incline. You roll the ball up the alley and try to get it into various sized holes. The smaller the hole, the tougher the shot, and the higher the point value. You accumulate tickets based on your score which can be traded in for prizes. Typically, there's a bank of Skee Ball lanes next to each other so many people can play at the same time. How well you do has no impact on anyone else. Everyone plays for their own results and generates results based on their level of skill. That's what the game of life is like.

Games have obstacles, things that are in the way of you winning. This requires you to develop and practice skills in order to overcome the obstacles and win. So does the game of life. While you are not playing the game of life against other people, you do have an opponent, or nemesis, working against you in the game of life. Your opponent didn't start out working against you. Quite the opposite, your opponent was originally created to help you. Somewhere along the line, much like Frankenstein's monster, their good intentions were corrupted and they stopped helping you and actually started to limit you and run your life and create whatever it is you don't want that you are currently experiencing in your life.

This may all sound rather insidious and a bit far fetched. Who is this villain that has taken over control of your life without you even realizing it? I call her Polly. Don't let the name fool you, calling her Polly may make her sound sweet and innocent, but she is no joke. Polly is sneaky, underhanded, manipulative and able to control you completely and subvert your creative power. Not only do you never see her coming, you don't even know she exists.

Polly is the name I give to my program. Now, before anyone takes offense, I would like to make it clear that I am not a misogynist. I have a mother, a wife, three daughters and 2 granddaughters. I love them and I like women. It was two friends of mine, Denise and Nancy, both women, who first introduced me to the name Polly. That was how they both referred to their program. I liked it so I stole, I mean borrowed, it for myself. It doesn't mean anything. When you think of your nemesis,or program, you can think of it as her or him or it. You can call your villain Polly, the Dark Overlord, Clyde, the Malevolent Tyrant or whatever works for you.

You know that your subconscious creates associations and beliefs based on your experiences and the information you get from your senses. These associations and beliefs are created to help your conscious mind process the repetitive sensory information you receive. Why take up valuable conscious processing power to figure out the same sensory input every time you encounter it? Instead, associations and beliefs can be used to handle the situation without conscious thought. How many times a day does someone ask you "How are you?". Do you think about the question before you answer it, or do you say the same thing in response, over and over again, like "I'm good, thanks, how are you?"

The same thinking was behind the creation of Computer Numeric Controlled, or CNC machines, for manufacturing. A company needs to create one thousand of the same item, let's say a chair leg. You put the raw material, a block of wood, into the machine, press a button and it does whatever is necessary to result in a chair leg. As long as you keep feeding it the raw material it will keep creating chair legs, all of which will be identical.

The chair leg is the result of a program that runs on the CNC machine. The program knows what tools to use, what operations to perform and in what order they need to be done to create the chair leg. It doesn't have to figure it out every time. When you put in a block of wood and press the button the program will generate the same result, a chair leg identical to all the other chair legs created by that program.

Your associations and beliefs are like the program a CNC machine uses. When an association or belief is triggered by something you see, hear, feel, taste or smell, it sets off a predetermined series of thoughts, emotions and actions that generate the same results every time.

"Would you like a cupcake?"
"I would, thank you." Munch, munch. "Mmmmm."
That was delicious and now I feel awesome. Cupcakes are great! No conscious mind processing required.

You create associations and beliefs all your life. They serve a useful purpose, helping the conscious mind process all the information it receives from your senses. When an association or belief is triggered, it can be handled without conscious processing. It takes over creation of the thoughts, emotions and actions that generate your results. Since it runs the same way every time, like a program, it generates the same results every time.

Somewhere along the line, your numerous and varied programs created this being I call Polly. It happened organically, as your conscious mind relied more and more on your associations and beliefs, your programs. It's like running on autopilot. Before you knew it, and without realizing it, you had turned a lot of control of your life over to Polly.

Wait a minute, the programs that comprise Polly are associations and beliefs that your subconscious created to help your conscious mind. So they're helpful programs, what's the problem with that?

There is no problem if all your associations and beliefs are supportive and empowering. The Real and Authentic You is amazing. The Real You lives in the moment, has unlimited potential and limitless possibilities. The Real You is connected to the Universe and knows how to create whatever you desire. The Real You does not judge, manipulate, or seek to have power and control over others. The Real You is loving and accepting and happy. If the Real and Authentic You created all your associations and beliefs - what I'm calling your programming - you are probably totally awesome. You're also probably not reading this book about getting more of what you want, having a better life and being happy because you're already creating all that you desire.

For most people, that's not what happened. Your associations and beliefs were created without any conscious thought, discretion or analysis. Things that you heard, saw and experienced in your conscious mind were passed on to your subconscious mind which accepted them and used them to create your associations and beliefs.

You are constantly bombarded with sensory input that your mind tries to figure out and uses to create associations and beliefs. There is no filter, or way to control the quality of what your senses are exposed to. When you're young, you have not yet developed a high capacity for reasoning and logical thinking. So much of your sensory input is simply accepted as it appears and associations and beliefs are created without any reasoning being involved. As a result, a lot of the associations and beliefs, or programs, that you create are based on other people's disempowering and limiting associations and beliefs.

Another interesting aspect is that there is no consistency as to how the mind connects things up. Similar situations may create different associations in your mind and people experiencing the same situation can each create different associations in their minds.

If you're a fan of science fiction, you know that nothing good ever happens when computer programs gain control over humans and get a bit of self-awareness. Think of H.A.L. 9000 from *2001: A Space Odyssey*, Skynet from *The Terminator* or Mr. Smith from *The Matrix*. This is what happened with Polly. Once she took over running most of your life she decided she liked it. Her focus went from supporting you to having power and control over you and self-preservation.

Polly is the reason why you keep getting the same results in your life. You believe that you don't know how to create different results or that you are powerless and unable to do anything different. That is how Polly maintains power and control over you and insures her continued existence.

To get more of what you want, have a better life and be happy, you must learn how to beat Polly at her own game. Have you ever set and followed through on a New Year's resolution? If you have, you're in the minority. Failed resolutions are the fodder for many a joke. Gyms and health clubs see a big surge in membership and attendance in January, most of which is gone by February. Why is that?

One of the main reasons is perception. A common perception of personal development, which is what a New Year's resolution is, is that it's hard. It's difficult to change who you are. That is a misconception. Change is something you were designed to do. Look at who you are now compared to who you were when you were born. You're completely different. Each decade of your life has probably seen significant changes in who you are. Even if it were true, and it's not, the Real You is capable of creating anything you desire. There is no need to change who you are, you are awesome. It's your programming that's creating the results in your life that you want to change. You don't need to change who you are, you simply have to reprogram yourself. That seems pretty easy. If you consider it a game, where you get to have the results you want by beating Polly, not only is it easy, it's fun.

Other reasons why resolutions don't work include lack of a plan, lack of discipline, weak mental muscles and disempowering beliefs and associations. I'll talk about those, as well as perceptions, later in this book.

Your thoughts, emotions and actions are always creating results. That's the game, creating results. You are always playing the game, whether you realize it or not. Everything you desire is a result. Focusing and directing your thoughts, emotions and actions is how you create the desired result. Are your results being created purposefully and with intent? If not, then Polly is creating the results in your life. Every time Polly creates a result that you did not necessarily choose or want, she wins and you lose. When you get in the game and learn how to beat Polly, you will start to create the results you choose and desire. At that point you will get more of what you want, have a better life and be happy. Polly loses and you win.

Be aware of the game. You are always in the game, playing for the desired result. Let's say your goal is to get up, get ready and leave the house by 7:30 AM. That's the result you're playing for, leaving the house at 7:30. The game is to get everything done by then. When your alarm goes off you start playing the game. Do you hit the snooze button or jump out of bed? Do you take a short or long shower? Getting yourself dressed, getting your kids ready, making and eating breakfast, and anything else that needs to be done before you leave is all part of the game. If you leave the house on time, you win. If you don't Polly wins. Either way, you get to play again tomorrow morning.

No matter what you are doing, you are always in the game playing for the desired result. Get clear about the results you are playing for. Being **consciously** focused on the results you are playing for increases your chances of winning the game.

Chapter Three

Why You're Losing The Game

When you're playing a game, it's helpful to know all you can about your opponent. In sports, this is known as scouting and teams spend a lot of time and effort to learn as much as they can before they play against the other team. Learning about their strengths and weaknesses helps to create a plan to counteract their strengths and exploit their weaknesses. This is your scouting report to support you in winning the game against Polly.

You win when you create the result you desire. That's what you're playing for, the result. What result is Polly playing for? Polly is playing for the status quo. Her goal is to have you run the same programs you've been running so that you continue to create the same results you've been getting. She doesn't want you to create a different result and she doesn't care what you want. Her survival is based on you running the same programs over and over, giving her power and control over you and insuring her continued existence.

Up to this point in your life, Polly's greatest trick was to remain hidden. If a murder looks like an accident, or death by natural causes, and no one suspects foul play, no one is looking for a perpetrator. That's how Polly has been able to hide in plain sight. Since you didn't know about Polly, you've believed that you are in control and generating the results in your life. You've always been playing the game against Polly, you just didn't know it. I told you Polly was sneaky.

So, the first skill for you to develop is awareness. Be aware that you are always in the game playing against Polly to create the results you desire. You also need to be aware of the tricks Polly employs to give her an advantage when she plays the game. I call these tricks of hers:

WMDs - Weapons of Mass Dysfunction

Polly's first Weapon of Mass Dysfunction is reality. As Robin Williams used to say, "Reality, what a concept".

Reality is defined as something that exists independently of ideas concerning it. Look around you. I'm sure there are objects with your reach. Go ahead and pick one of them up. It's real, it exists, you can see it and touch it. You can smell it and shake it to see if it makes any sound. You can also lick it, but I'd be a little more cautious about that if I were you. It's real and a part of what we call the real world. Up to this point, the object you picked up has existed independently of any ideas concerning it. It is what it is and you have simply used your senses to observe it.

Now, I want you to tell me what the object is. Bazinga! As soon as you name it, describe it, or communicate about it in any way, reality has left the building and you are in the realm of perception. You have taken what is real and interpreted it. The words you use to describe it are not the object. The object is what it is. When you think about it or describe it, that is your perception or interpretation of the object, it is not the actual object.

I see you rolling your eyes right now. You're probably thinking "So what? Who cares? What difference does it make?" Oh baby, it actually makes all of the difference in the world.

Reality is interpreted through your past experiences and the associations and beliefs your mind has created and the result is your perception of reality. Guess who's controlling your perception of reality? That's right, Polly filters your perception through all of your programming to create the perception that supports her results, not yours.

To further complicate things, everyone else does the same thing. What they see and hear is filtered through their programming and they arrive at their own perception of reality.

The result is that everyone thinks their perception is reality, when the reality is that everyone lives within their perception, and no two people have the same perception about everything. Therefore, everyone's perceived reality is different.

This is not an issue when perceptions are in agreement or alignment, but it becomes a major issue when perceptions differ. Each individual is convinced that their perception is reality when the reality is that their perception is simply an interpretation and there are an infinite number of possible interpretations.

This can be confusing so let me reiterate. Reality is the world as it exists without any ideas concerning it. It is what it is. You, like everyone else in the world, perceive reality filtered through your own unique combination of experiences, associations and beliefs. That is not reality, that is your perception of reality. Everyone's perception of reality is different and none of them are real, they are all perceptions or interpretations. Since no person's perception is reality, no person's perception is any more or less valid than anyone else's, they're just different. And none of them are reality.

WMD # 1 - Your Perception is Not Reality

If you understand that your thoughts, associations and beliefs are simply your perception of reality - and that your perception is no more or less valid than my perception, which may be different from yours - then you can simply accept that we have different perceptions. That's what the two-year-old Real and Authentic You could do without any problems. You could share your thoughts with your friends and they could share their thoughts with you and nobody cared if your perceptions were the same or different. You accepted their perceptions as a valid viewpoint without any need to agree or disagree. There was no need to make anyone right or wrong, different perceptions were simply accepted.

Doesn't that sound awesome? A world where people can have different perceptions, beliefs and associations and where all those different thoughts and ideas can coexist and be accepted. Unfortunately, thanks to Polly making everyone think that their perception is reality, that's not the world we live in. As if that's not enough, Polly kicks it up a notch by expanding on perception to make up stories. Wait, seems like that should be a bigger deal.

WMD # 2 - Stories

There we go, that's better. Did you ever play the game telephone? A bunch of people sit in a circle. The first person whispers a sentence to the person next to them. That person is supposed to whisper the exact same sentence to the person sitting next to them. This continues from person to person, all around the circle, until the last person passes it back to the person who started the process. Invariably, by the time it gets to the last person, the sentence that was supposed to be repeated exactly has changed completely.

This is an example of how susceptible to misinterpretation communication is. Miscommunication happens all the time and it's really no surprise. Thoughts can be very complex things that include pictures, words, feelings, tastes and smells. To communicate all of that with only words can be very difficult. Words are subject to interpretation. If you ask ten people to name and describe a vehicle, chances are good you'll get ten different responses. Words can be imprecise and they are subject to interpretation by both the sender and the receiver of the communication.

Other factors also impact communication. If the receiver is distracted, or simply not paying attention, they might miss part of the communication and make up words to fill in the blanks. The mental state of both parties affects what is said, what is heard and how it is interpreted. Nonverbal cues, like body language and facial expressions, also influence how a communication is interpreted. Chances are good you've experienced this both as a sender and a receiver. In other words, you've misinterpreted what someone said to you and had someone you were speaking to misinterpret what you said.

What does Polly do with all this fuzzy communication? She makes up stories. Polly is an amazing storyteller. She can spin a yarn out of nothing and convince you it's real without breaking a sweat. Polly puts made up stories in your mind all the time.

When someone speaks, what's real is that someone says something. Everything that follows is interpretation. Your interpretation of what someone says is not real, it's a story. Someone says "I'm angry" to you. Your programming hears the words and considers the tonality, nonverbal cues like facial expressions and posture, previous communications, your overall perception of this person and a multitude of other factors and makes up a story about what was said and what it means. You might think "What did I do to make them angry?", or "You're always angry about something", or "Oh no, do they know I did such and such?"

You never really know what anyone else is thinking or means by what they say. Verbal communication is subject to much confusion and misinterpretation; words don't necessarily mean the same thing to everyone; verbal cues like sarcasm can be missed. People intentionally misdirect, omit, exaggerate, stretch the truth, tell half-truths and outright lie all the time. Not necessarily maliciously, maybe to spare someone's feelings or to avoid having to explain themselves. Regardless, Polly takes in this sensory information and makes up stories to support your programming.

Just as your perception is not reality, your interpretation of what other people say and do is really just a story.

WMD # 3 - Judgment

Judgment is about right and wrong, good and bad. Judgment is why Polly must first convince you that your perception is reality. If you believe that everyone is entitled to their own perception, and that perceptions can be different and coexist, then there is no judgment, there's acceptance. There also isn't right or wrong, good or bad. Those are judgments based on perception. On the other hand, if you believe your perception is reality, and my perception is different than yours, then your program gets to make itself right and me wrong. You being right and me being wrong gives your program the appearance of power and control. I say appearance of power and control because there is no right or wrong, there are simply two different perceptions. However, if my program buys into the concept of perception equals reality, which is the basis for judgment, then it will also perceive you being right as you having power over me.

For this to work, we both have to believe that our perceptions are reality and that differing perceptions can't coexist. Luckily, I'm as programmed as you are and my programs are running me, just like your programs are running you, just like everyone else's program is running them, so we're all playing the same stupid game of judgment.

Good and bad, right and wrong are not real. They are judgments based on your perceptions.

WMD # 4 - Blame

Polly loves this WMD. Blame is about fault and making people wrong. Fault, right and wrong are not real, they are perceptions based on judgment. Polly uses blame to reassign or avoid responsibility.

How do you feel when someone blames you for something? Don't you feel like you're being attacked? This makes you defensive. Maybe you decide to retaliate and blame the other person, or a third person, or events outside of your control. Once blame is assigned, power and control over that person is achieved.

The concept of blame, of reassigning responsibility, is flawed. Responsibility is always present and it rests with the person whose actions created the result. It's a simple case of cause and effect. You are responsible for your words and actions and their consequences. Responsibility cannot be reassigned after the fact.

Polly uses the belief that your perception is reality, the stories she makes up, judgment and blame to control your thoughts, emotions, and actions, to continue to generate the same results in your life.

Let's look at a common New Year's resolution, getting healthy. You, the Real and Authentic You, wants to lose weight and get in shape. Polly wants you to keep doing what you've been doing; not exercising and eating all kinds of foods that don't support good health. You know, the ones that taste good and trigger the pleasure centers in your brain, like sugary and salty snacks.

You commit to eating better and join a gym. Day one you make a salad for lunch and go to the gym after work. Maybe you do that for a couple of days. Then Polly starts to put thoughts in your head to sabotage your efforts.

"It's hard to make a salad every day."
"Having fast food one day won't kill me."
"I had to work late, I don't have time to go to the gym."
"My life is so busy, I deserve to go to happy hour."
"Getting healthy is hard, I can't do it, waaaaah!"

Before you know it, Polly has filled your mind with her perception of realty, made up stories, tossed in a healthy dose of judgment and blame and you've given up on your New Year's resolution and are doing the exact same thing you were doing; sitting on the couch and eating junk food. Which is exactly the result Polly was playing for.

Thinking your perception is reality, making up stories, being judgmental and blaming others are how you'll know when Polly shows up and is playing against you.

Chapter Four

How The Game is Played

Like everyone else, you create associations and beliefs and then run them like programs. This is what is creating the results in your life. If you want to create different results in your life, get more of what you want, have a better life and be happy, you must break out of the patterns that your programmatic behavior is creating. So it's important for you to be able to recognize programmatic thoughts and behavior.

Not all of your programs are disempowering and limiting. A lot of them are empowering and supportive. You may have noticed that I've been focusing on the disempowering and limiting associations and beliefs. The reason is simple; the empowering and supportive programs are not the ones keeping you from having what you want and being happy. So when I talk about Polly, I'm talking about the disempowering and limiting associations and beliefs that are creating the results you don't want in your life. When your programming supports you, feel free to sit back and enjoy the ride.

How do you know when Polly is putting non-supportive, programmatic thoughts in your mind? It's probably happening quite a lot. Pay attention to the thoughts in your head. If you did not put them there consciously, they are coming from your programming. Here are some thoughts to be on the lookout for.

- Feeling anxious or stressed. Emotions are a result of your thoughts. Feelings you don't enjoy experiencing, like anxiety and stress, are created by programmatic thoughts from Polly.

- Thoughts like "I can't" or "I'm overwhelmed". The Real You is amazing and able to create anything you desire. Disempowering and limiting thoughts come from Polly.

- Judgmental thoughts like right and wrong, good and bad. All your judgmental thoughts come from programming. The Real You is accepting and loving.

- Thinking your perception is reality. That comes from programming and typically leads to judgmental thoughts.

- A desire to control someone else's thoughts or behavior.

You know what programmatic behavior is, you've just called it something else. Here's a list of some common programs that people run.

Victim	Tyrant
Controlling / Bossy	Manipulative
Self-Righteous	Know It All
Not good enough	Worthless
Doormat	Defensive
Insecure	Indecisive
Enabler	Arrogant
Irresponsible	Anxious
Unlovable	Inadequate
Angry	Judgmental
Selfish	Scared

You've probably seen each of these programs running at one time or another in other people. You run them as well, although you seldom recognize it when you do. That's how Polly hides in plain sight. When you run one of these programs, you don't realize it's a program. You think it's you having the thoughts that create the emotions and actions and generate the results you are experiencing in your life when it's really Polly.

While you run many different programs all day long, there are some of them that you run more often. These are the programs that define who you are to other people. For instance, you probably run victim at some point or another. Almost everybody feels the need for a little pity party now and again. That doesn't necessarily make victim one of your core programs. When someone runs victim as a core program you can tell from their withdrawn posture, like they expect to be hit at any moment. Their gaze is down, voice is soft, and it looks like life beats up on them on a regular basis.

Are you able to categorize people you know with a word or two? I know I hear it all the time, someone being called a control freak, know it all, doormat, wishy-washy, judgmental or irresponsible, for example. Congratulations, if you're able to categorize other people with a word or two, chances are good you have identified one or two of their core programs.

While it's interesting to identify the specific programs that you and others run, it's not necessary in order to generate new results in your life. The goal is to recognize programmatic thoughts and behaviors and choose a different thought to prevent or interrupt the programmatic response.

To understand this, let's look at what happens when a program runs. We are continuously experiencing sensory input. Sensory input consists of the things we see, hear, smell, taste and feel. The conscious mind must process all that sensory input to figure out what it means and what, if anything you should do. You are continuously creating associations and beliefs so that you don't have to consciously process the sensory data. Your associations and beliefs are triggered when you encounter the previously processed sensory data. Think of the cupcake example from Chapter 1.

Once your senses trigger the association, the program runs. The program consists of the thoughts, emotions and actions that you previously associated with the sensory input, the trigger. You think "I like cupcakes, yum!", you feel happy imagining the texture and taste, and you peel off the paper and take a big bite. Every time you encounter a cupcake you go through the same sequence of thought, emotion and action that generates the same result. You eat the cupcake and feel happy.

What if you decide you want to lose some weight? Is eating the cupcake supportive of that result? Not at all. But the force is strong in Polly. She'll have you eating that cupcake before you even realize what you're doing. Then you'll feel regret and shame and be unhappy. But it's too late, Polly has already generated the result for you, a result the Real You didn't want or choose. Game to Polly, she wins and you lose. Play again.

In order to generate a different result, you must interrupt the program at some point before the result you don't want is generated. You can replace the "I like cupcakes, yum!" thought with "Nothing tastes as good as thin feels. I am committed to losing weight." Or any other thought that supports the result You desire, losing weight. When you change your thoughts, you change your emotions, because your emotions are a result of your thoughts. You'll start to feel bad when you think about eating the cupcake. Finally, the new thoughts and emotions will create a different result, you'll choose to not eat the cupcake. That game goes to you. You win, Polly loses. Every time you encounter a cupcake you get to play that same game.

Here's another example. I'll use road rage, a program I run often and with which I am intimately familiar. This is a game I get to play all the time.

I am a very focused driver. When I get behind the wheel of a car I am totally present to what is going on around me. My goal is to get from point A to point B as quickly and efficiently as possible. When driving on the highway, I like to engage the cruise control and relax. I stay to the right except to pass and, when I do pull out to pass, I do so quickly and move over so I'm not in the way of other drivers going faster than me. I have many more rules about driving and I want other drivers to follow my rules and drive the same way I do.

That is a setup for a disempowering programmatic response, the desire to control other people's behavior. Based on my observations, very few people have the same rules and drive the same way I do. Invariably, another driver is going to do something that is not in alignment with my programmatic beliefs about driving. Let's say I'm cruising along in the left-hand lane and someone pulls out in front of me and they're going slower than I am, so I have to hit the brakes. That's the trigger, Polly is off and running.

First come the programmatic thoughts. "What an asshole!", "You don't know how to drive!", "Why would you pull out right in front of me like that?", "What the hell were you thinking?", and other thoughts that include a lot of "Effing this" and "Effing that". My thoughts are full of judgment, making me right and them wrong.

41

These thoughts immediately generate an emotion; I get angry. I mean stupid angry, irrationally angry, want to pull out a gun and shoot you angry. I want to let them know how pissed off I am and teach them a lesson so they won't do that again. So I lean on the horn, flip them the bird, maybe flash my headlights. If I have an opportunity to get around them I do so, pulling in dangerously close ahead of them and possibly flipping them off again. Maybe I'll tap my brakes to get them to brake and shake them up. Yes, I am that asshole you don't want anywhere near you when you're driving. When all that happens it's game to Polly.

This is a programmatic response I work on a lot. The work starts with the programmatic thoughts. I notice when Polly starts putting them in my mind and choose to let them go and think other thoughts. I might think "Mark, the reality is they're ahead of you and there's nothing you can do, so chill." Or think about how ridiculous the programmatic thoughts are. "What would you think if someone told you a person was shot simply for pulling out in front of someone on the highway? Can you imagine having to admit doing that to their spouse and kids? Do you really want to be that guy?" Or "They're probably not even aware of what they did. Good thing I'm paying attention." Or I might take a deep breath and simply tell myself "Let it go, Mark."

When I recognize the programmatic thoughts, and choose to replace them with different thoughts, I don't get angry or engage in any of the stupid angry behaviors. I back off, give them room and wait for them to pull over. If they don't pull over, I'll wait for a safe place to pass them and do it without any of the other programmatic stupid angry actions. That game goes to me.

Sometimes I'm triggered and the thoughts occur and generate the emotions and actions before I have a chance to recognize what's happening and change the thoughts. I can still change the thoughts and change the results at any point before the programmatic response has completed. I can be angry, change my thoughts and let go of the anger before I do something stupid. I can even start to do something stupid, like hit the gas and prepare to pull out around them, change my thoughts and let go of the programmatic behavior, letting off the gas and giving them room. I win that game as well.

So that's how the game is played. Polly has a sequence of thoughts, emotions and actions for every trigger. Every time a specific trigger occurs she runs that sequence, generating the same result every time. When she does that, she wins and you lose. For you to win, you must recognize the programmatic thought, consciously choose a different thought to replace the programmatic thought, and generate a different result based on the new thoughts, emotions and actions. When you do that, you win the game. More importantly, you start to get more of what you want, have a better life and be happy.

Sounds simple, right? Well, it is. Be aware and change your thoughts. The challenge is that your typical day is full of triggers and programmatic responses. You get triggered by your spouse, partner, kid, boss, employee, coworkers, the news, weather, traffic and millions of other bits of sensory input you receive every day. Each trigger ignites its own programmatic response. When triggered, each programmatic response generates the same thoughts in your mind, which create the same emotions and actions and which generate the same results every time. Your programmatic response will vary based on the trigger. However, when invoked, a programmatic response runs the same way every time. You have to admire Polly's consistency. It's not unusual for you to spend a lot of your day being triggered and going from one programmatic response to the next.

Pay attention to what's happening around you and in your head and you will be amazed. Different triggers generate different programmatic responses. Programs run big and small. Polly is very creative and has lots of programs for you to run. When you get triggered, notice the thoughts in your head. Where did those thoughts come from? Polly, of course. Polly has been running the show for a long time and she's really good at it. So good that you think those are your thoughts, rather than thoughts generated by your programming to control you and your life.

That's the game you and Polly play every day. Now you know how the game is played, how you win and how Polly wins.

Chapter Five

How To Create Different Results

The biggest obstacle you face in creating all that you desire is Polly. She likes things just the way they are. Polly is also very good at the game. She's been winning at the game most of your life, while you didn't even know you were playing. Polly is an expert at maintaining the status quo. That's why your results have remained the same, even though you desired something different. If you want to generate different results you have to get in the game. Now that you know there's a game, and who you're playing against, you can recognize the truth in this quote attributed to Albert Einstein:

Insanity: doing the same thing over and over again, expecting different results.

Whether or not Einstein actually said this, you don't need to be a genius to understand the truth in that statement. It's basic cause and effect. Hit your thumb with a hammer and it's going to hurt, every time. Put your hand on a hot stove burner and you're going to get burned, every time. To keep hitting your thumb or touching the hot burner and expecting a different result is crazy. I mean, really nuts.

I enjoy bowling. When I was young, twelve to sixteen, I used to bowl in a league on Saturday mornings. I loved the feeling of the ball releasing perfectly off my hand and the sound of it rolling smoothly down the lane, curving in to hit the head pin. I loved hearing the crash of the pins as the ball struck them, and the sight of the pins exploding away as the ball smashed through them. Bowling has a single, simple desired result; knock down all the pins, ideally on your first ball. That's called a strike, ten up and then ten down, as a result of your well-placed ball.

The basic idea is to roll your ball down the alley to the side of the head pin. If you're right handed, you use your wrist to spin the ball and get it to curve into the sweet spot right between the head pin and the number three pin, behind and to the right of the head pin. You want the spin, known as putting action on the ball, to really get the pins flying, which significantly increases your chances of getting a strike.

There are many factors that influence how many pins go down when your ball hits them. It's very easy to throw a ball that looks good but doesn't get the desired result. The most heartbreaking result is a well-placed ball with lots of action that leaves one pin standing. When that would happen, we would say "Oh well, shoot for nine and you get nine". We knew that no matter how good the ball looked going down the alley and hitting the pins, all that really mattered was the result. If the result was nine pins knocked down instead of ten, then obviously, the shot, regardless of how it looked and felt when you threw it, was only a nine pin shot, not a strike.

You see, the results don't lie. So, if insanity is doing the same thing over and over again and expecting different results, then getting the same results means you're not doing anything differently, even if you think you are. Results don't lie.

When it comes to creating, your thoughts, emotions and actions are the cause, and the results you generate are the effects. Polly's goal with programming is to get you to have the same thoughts, emotions and actions every time that program runs so you generate the same results. If you want different results, you're going to have to create different thoughts, emotions and actions. That's how you get in the game.

Like water and electricity, you follow the path of least resistance. You may not be happy with the results you're getting, but what you're doing to get these results feels very familiar to you. Continuing to do what you've been doing is comfortable.

Comfortable is like kryptonite to change. Change isn't comfortable. Change involves doing something different than what you've been doing. That's going to be uncomfortable. It's going to feel weird. When that happens, Polly is going to put thoughts in your head like "I can't do this." And "It's too hard."

That's bull dookey and you must recognize it as such. The challenge is recognizing that those programmatic, disempowering and limiting thoughts come from Polly, not from the Real You. Those thoughts are Polly using her WMDs, Weapons of Mass Dysfunction. Hard and easy are perceptions, they are not real. There is no hard or easy, there's only do or not do. Either you will do something different to create a different result or you won't do something different and continue to generate the same result you don't want. That's Polly using WMD #1, convincing you that your perception is reality when it's not, it's simply a perception. Remember, you're creating all the time. Creating what you want is no harder than creating what you don't want. That's simply a perception Polly uses to control you.

Then Polly is going to make up stories and put them in your mind. These stories will be full of reasons and rationalizations as to why you can't do anything different, or why you need to procrastinate and put off doing anything different. You'll think these stories are real. Your life is too busy, your kids or parents need your help, you're too tired, you'll do it tomorrow. When tomorrow gets here Polly is going to put the same disempowering and limiting thoughts in your head and convince you that you're committed to getting started on changing your life tomorrow. That's a story, she's lying to you, tomorrow doesn't exist. The only time in which you can change your thoughts, emotions and actions to create a different result is NOW. Tomorrow is smoke and mirrors, Polly's way to maintain control and get you to keep creating the same results.

Then she'll throw in some WMD #3, judgment. She'll put thoughts in your head like "This won't work. This is stupid. I can't. My life isn't so bad. Lots of people have it worse than me. Change is hard, staying the same is easier." No, it's not really easier, that's a judgment call based on perception, Polly's perception. It is comfortable, and the price of comfort is a guarantee that nothing in your life will change. No more, no better, no happy.

Finally, Polly uses WMD #4, blame, to knock you out of the game before you're even in it. If Polly convinces you that it's someone else's fault that you don't have what you want in your life, then there's no reason for you to do something different because it won't matter. You can't create a different result, only some person or event outside of your control can do that. So just keep on doing what you've been doing. It's comfortable and easy and besides, you're powerless to create a different result and get what you want.

That's just more programmatic bull dookey and now you know it.

Polly can be seductive or a real bitch, depending on what it takes to get her way. Carrot or stick, she has no shame and will stop at nothing to derail your attempts to take back control of your life.

Don't let her.

Another thought Polly will put in your head is "It doesn't matter." Maybe it's that the programmatic thought in your head in this moment doesn't matter so there's no reason to play the game and change it. Or that the result you generated is no big deal, so having the programmatic response doesn't matter.

The truth is, IT ALL MATTERS! It's all connected. How do you get better at something? You get better through repetition. Repetition is the mother of skill, as Tony Robbins says. Why do athletes practice the basic skills of their sport over and over again? So that, when they're playing the game, they can use their skill to execute the play that helps win the game.

How are you going to get better at playing the game if you don't practice? That's easy, you're not. So you practice recognizing and changing programmatic thoughts every chance you get. When you do that, you generate different emotions and actions and create different results. Game to you, and you just got better at playing the game. It's easier to do when you're playing for small results and that supports you when you're playing for big results.

Polly doesn't want you to practice and get better at playing and winning the game so she tries to convince you that it doesn't matter. But, it does. Be aware and play the game as often as possible.

One final note. This book cannot change your life. No book can change your life. A book can provide you with information and allow you to learn from someone else's efforts and mistakes. It can be a wonderful tool if properly understood and used by YOU to change your life.

Francis Bacon was an English philosopher who wrote:

Knowledge is power.

When I first read this quote of his, I agreed with it. Over the years I have gained more knowledge by studying personal development. I have come to recognize that knowledge is **potential** power. Knowing more did not generate different results in my life. My results changed when I aced based on my knowledge. So, it's really the **application of knowledge that has power**.

For instance, knowing how to build a rocket ship has the potential to land a man on the moon. Actually building a rocket ship, launching a man into space and landing him on the moon allows him to do a real moon walk, not the Michael Jackson version. So, while knowledge is an important component of the process, it's action that generates a result.

This is an important distinction. Reading a book, no matter how great that book is, won't change your life. It's only by acting on the information contained in the book that your life will change.

Only through action can you change your life

Your thoughts have the power of creation and You have the ability to create anything You desire with your thoughts. Creation does not happen spontaneously. In order to create you must take action. This is the Law of Cause of Effect. Actions are the cause and the effects are the results you get.

YOU MUST TAKE ACTION TO GET IN THE GAME

Chapter Six

How To Win The Game

When you decide to take back control of your life from Polly, be prepared; she is going to fight you every step of the way. Polly wants to survive. Survival for Polly is being able to run her programming to control your life. When you decide to take back control of your life, Polly views that as death to her. Polly is mean; she plays dirty; and she will do anything to survive.

At this point you might be thinking that in order to take back control of your life you must eliminate Polly, get rid of your programming. That's not how it works. You can't get rid of programming. Remember, programs come from associations and beliefs that your subconscious mind creates to help your conscious mind. Programming is how your mind works and you can't get rid of it.

However, there are things you can do to beat Polly at her own game. One is to recognize the programmatic thoughts, emotions and actions in the moment when they occur, and to choose other thoughts that will create new emotions and actions generating a different result. In the example of road rage, I showed you how, when you are triggered, Polly puts in your mind the disempowering thoughts that will create the same emotions and actions and generate the same results every time. I then showed you how to interrupt that process by choosing different thoughts in the moment.

The second way to beat Polly is to reprogram yourself with

perceptions, associations and beliefs that will support and empower you. Your programs were generated without conscious thought, planning or focus on your part. Your subconscious mind created them as a result of the sensory input you received. Much of that input came from other people and included their perceptions, stories, judgment, blame and other disempowering and limiting beliefs and associations. Your conscious mind was not developed enough to filter and check the validity of this input so it all was used by your subconscious in creating your associations, perceptions and beliefs.

As with any game, there are basic skills to learn and develop that will increase your ability to play the game. This chapter looks at the skills that will support you in reprogramming yourself with empowering and supportive associations, beliefs and perceptions to help you win the game against Polly.

Associations

Associations are links your mind made between your sensory input and your thoughts, emotions and actions, like the cupcake association I described earlier. Most of your disempowering associations were not created consciously. One way to reprogram a disempowering association is to consciously choose a new association.

I like coffee. Don't even try to talk to me in the morning before I have my first cup of hot coffee. The coffee, while hot when I pour it, cools off over time. It used to be that when I took a sip of that cold coffee I would go "Yuck" and throw the rest of it out. I didn't like cold coffee. One day someone asked me if I liked iced coffee. I replied "Why yes, I do." I was then asked "What's the difference between iced coffee and the cold coffee you just threw out?" My head spun around and smoke came out of my ears as I realized there wasn't really any difference at all. Iced coffee may be a bit colder, but it's basically the same thing as hot coffee which has grown cold. By changing my perception and creating a new association, I now enjoy my coffee no matter what temperature it is.

Many of your associations and beliefs are easily replaced by simply deciding to create a new one. These are the ones that don't have a lot of repetition or emotion wrapped around them. Polly is not that vested in maintaining them because she doesn't consider them to be that important in maintaining control over you. I call these the low hanging fruit, easy to pick. These small victories will help to build your capacity and ability to challenge Polly on the bigger issues.

Fear

Fear is a response to perceived danger. A perceived threat can trigger the fight or flight response. This was very useful in allowing humans to survive and work their way to the top of the food chain. Today, most people do not face threats to their survival on a daily basis. In fact, you might go through your whole life without ever encountering a life-threatening event.

Yet that fear mechanism still exists within us. Polly uses that fear against you when she plays the game. "I'm afraid I'm going to lose my job." "I'm afraid I'm going to flunk my class." Sometimes she tempers the fear talk and uses worry, or anxiety, or uncertainty, or distress. Polly can get you to feel that way about anything and everything.

All those things that you're afraid of, worried about, anxious, uncertain or distressed over are simply results. If you get a result other than the one you were playing for, what do you get to do?

You get to play again. The best way to avoid a result you don't want is to focus on the result you do want. If you're worried about losing your job, do your job so well that your employer would have to be an idiot to fire you. If they're downsizing and your job is being phased out, be such a good worker your boss wants to find another position for you so they don't lose you. If you do lose your job, make sure you were so good at your job that someone else will want to hire you.

How effective will you be at your job if you're afraid, worried, anxious, uncertain or distressed all day long? If your focus is on losing your job, what result are you going to generate?

I think Zig Ziglar said it best when he stated that fear was an acronym for:
False
Evidence
Appearing
Real.

When Polly is filling your mind with thoughts of fear, worry, anxiety, uncertainty, or distress, ask yourself what imagined result is creating those emotions. Understand and accept that imagined result is a possibility. Then decide what result you desire and are going to play for and get in the game and do everything you can to create your desired result.

Failure

One of the biggest fears driving programmatic behavior is the fear of failure. You may have been conditioned to believe that failure is this big, bad, evil thing you should fear and avoid at all costs. You knew better when you were a toddler, learning to walk. How many times did you stumble and fall? Did that deter you? Of course not, you knew that repetition is the mother of skill and failure is it's father. So, you pulled yourself up and tried again. Failure is not a bad thing. Failure is simply a lack of success. All it means is that you didn't get the result you were playing for.

Thomas Edison knew this. He tried over 10,000 different materials for the filament in his quest to create the incandescent light bulb. When asked by a reporter how it felt to have failed over 10,000 times, he replied that he hadn't failed at all, he had successfully identified 10,000 things that didn't work. Reprogram yourself with the belief that the only failure lies in giving up. If you haven't given up on getting the result you want, then you haven't failed. You just didn't get the result you wanted and you get to play again. That's how you look at failure from an empowered, supportive viewpoint.

When you don't get the result you want, Polly will put thoughts in your mind like "I failed. I'm a failure. I can't do it. No reason to try, I'm a loser. I can't do anything." The disempowering thoughts will come fast and furious, followed closely by the emotions that support them which you don't enjoy and would prefer not to feel. As soon as that first thought of failure shows up, recognize and replace it. Think "I haven't failed, that's Polly talking. I simply didn't get the result I was playing for. So what? I get to play again for the result I want. And again, and again, and again, because the only failure lies in giving up. Whoo-hoo, I'm coming for you, Polly. Best be prepared to lose because I plan on winning this game!" These thoughts will make you feel happy and powerful, emotions you enjoy. The actions you take based on those thoughts and emotions will be in alignment with creating the results you desire. Game over, Polly. You win and she loses.

The challenge you face is that Polly has been controlling your thoughts for so long that you're out of practice. You might say your mental muscles are weak. You strengthen your mental muscles the same way you do your physical muscles, by using them and through repetition. Repetition is the mother of skill. Keep practicing, rinse and repeat, and your skill will increase and your mental muscles will get stronger. Here are some more perceptions, associations, beliefs and behaviors to support you in this process.

Life is a game

Tell yourself over and over yourself that life is a game. I've already spoken to this and repetition is the mother of skill. Keep focusing on your desired results. The desired result is what you're playing for. Games are fun, and if life is a game then life is fun. You don't fail at games, you just lose a game. When you do, you get to play again. As long as you keep playing you have a chance to win. No matter what game you are playing, you always have a desired result. Get clear about the results you are playing for. Being **consciously** focused on the results you are playing for increases your chances of winning the game.

Live in the Moment.

If you're like most people, your thoughts wander. Chances are good you spend a lot of time thinking about things that have nothing to do with the present moment. The party last weekend, picking up the kids after school, making dinner when you get home, what someone said yesterday, tomorrow's meeting, where you're going on vacation, not having enough money for vacation, and on, and on, and on. The list of things to think about is endless.

Is that controlling your thoughts? No, those thoughts aren't being generated consciously by you. They're coming from Polly. Getting more of what you want is a result of the actions you take. The only time you can take action is the moment of now. Actions are generated by your thoughts and emotions. To take action now, your thoughts and emotions must be present in the moment of now. Polly doesn't want you to be present in the moment and take control of your thoughts. She wants to control your thoughts so that she can control your life and your results. The result she's playing for is to keep things exactly the way they are.

Getting more of what you want, having a better life and being happy starts with taking back control of your thoughts. That is something that you do in the moment, every moment. To control your thoughts in the moment, you must be present in the moment. This is the game you're playing against Polly and it's happening all the time. Polly is very good at this game.

Control your thoughts.

This might seem a bit repetitive. If you think so, congratulations, you're paying attention. Why am I being repetitive? Because repetition is the mother of skill. My previous point was to be present in the moment so you **can** control your thoughts. Now I'm talking about **actually controlling** your thoughts. Your thoughts - the only thing in the Universe over which you have direct control - contain the power of creation. All you have to do in order to have everything you want in life is to control your thoughts. Sounds simple, right? Unfortunately, not so much.

Having the **ability** to control your thoughts doesn't mean you actually **do** control your thoughts. Remember all of that programming your subconscious mind created to help your conscious mind? Most of what you deal with day to day you've turned over to Polly. So your programs are generating the thoughts, emotions and actions in your life that are creating the results in your life. You're not controlling your thoughts, Polly is.

In fact, at this point she is way better at controlling your thoughts than you are. She's been doing it and is used to doing it. You're not. So what's going to happen when you attempt to control your thoughts? It's going to feel uncomfortable, allowing Polly to plant more thoughts to undermine you. As you work on taking back control of your life you will start to get used to being uncomfortable. That's when you know you can take action to generate a different result.

Your perception is not reality.

This is another belief that sounds simple and that Polly will do anything to prevent you from creating. Almost all her power stems from your belief that your perception IS reality. That provides the foundation for her to build her stories, be judgmental and play the blame game. Everything you think, feel and do is a result of how you perceive reality. Your perception is not reality, it's simply your interpretation. Whenever thinking or talking about anything outside of yourself add "It's my perception" or "My interpretation is" or "It seems to me" to the beginning of the sentence. This keeps you present to the fact that your thoughts, feelings and actions are based on your perception of reality and that your perception is not reality. Neither is anyone's else's perception reality so you can add the same words to what anyone says to you.

Acceptance

Acceptance starts with accepting yourself as you are. You, the Real You, are awesome and amazing and capable of achieving great things. You are not your programming. Getting more of what you want, having a better life and being happy is about moving beyond the programmatic thoughts, emotions and behaviors that are creating the results in your life that you don't want. Your life is a journey. As you travel along the path of your life you learn and change through your experiences. This changes your beliefs and associations, increasing your capacity to create the results you desire in your life.

Learn to accept how things are, not how you want them to be. Wishing things were different does not make them different. It is what it is. Refusing to accept what things are, allows Polly to generate thoughts, emotions and actions that support disempowering and limiting programs.

Accept that other people's thoughts are their perception and that their emotions and actions are a result of their perception. They are as entitled to their own perception as much as you are entitled to yours. Their perception does not have to agree with your perception. Neither your interpretation nor their interpretation is reality. When you learn to accept, you understand that there is no right or wrong, allowing you to move beyond judgment. Accept others for who they are.

Acceptance does not mean agreement. You can acknowledge that someone else has a perception that is different from yours and agree to disagree. Problems arise when someone confuses their perception with reality and tries to convince anyone who has a different perception that they are wrong. That's Polly working hard to maintain power and control.

When you accept how things are and what other people do and say, you can move beyond programmatic responses and choose the thoughts, emotions and actions that support the result you desire.

To support you in your goal of acceptance, commit to replacing all judgmental thoughts and words with one of these words; empowering, supportive, disempowering and limiting. Anything that moves you closer to what you want is empowering or supportive. Anything that does not move you closer to, or moves you away from what you want, is disempowering or limiting. Use those same words when thinking and talking about other people. Judgmental thoughts and words come from Polly. When you stop thinking and expressing in judgmental terms you weaken your programming and move closer to acceptance.

Let Go

Letting go is a corollary to acceptance. Polly is going to throw a lot of programmatic thoughts your way. These thoughts generate emotions and actions. When you recognize these programmatic thoughts you have the opportunity to let them go, freeing yourself from the cycle of programmatic thoughts, emotions, actions and results.

You may never be able to stop the programmatic thoughts from being generated by Polly. Even with all my years of work on my own personal development, I still have programmatic thoughts. Rather than trying to stop them, I am able to recognize them and choose a different thought. That means I have to let go of the programmatic thought. I mentioned this in my road rage example as one of the ways to move beyond my programmatic response.

Sounds simple, right? I picture the programmatic thought as a brightly colored balloon with a long string that I have lightly grasped in my hand. I decide to let it go and open my hand, expecting to see the balloon float gently away on the breeze. To my surprise, the balloon stays right where it is. I look down and see the string wrapped around Polly's hand. Her fist is clenched tightly around the string, holding on for dear life. Getting Polly to let go of the programmatic thought is like trying to pry open the fist of a five year old. Initially, it may seem like an almost impossible task.

Remember, repetition is the mother of skill. That's another way of saying "Practice makes perfect". When you first attempt to let go it may feel weird, awkward and uncomfortable. That's not real, those feelings are generated by thoughts put into your mind by Polly. She is attempting to derail your efforts to take back control of your life. Your ability to control your thoughts will strengthen and the programmatic feelings Polly creates will weaken as you repeatedly confront the programmatic thoughts and move beyond them to choose the thought that supports you in the moment.

Accept Responsibility

Polly is an expert at using blame to manipulate people, She loves to find fault, judge, and make everyone wrong - including you. When Polly uses blame to reassign responsibility to someone else, she is giving them the power to control your life. What chance do you have to get what you want in life if it's up to somebody else to give it to you? You have two chances, slim and none. No one else is looking out for you. They're all listening to the same radio station, WII-FM - What's In It For Me. If you're relying on someone or something else to provide you with all that you desire, you better get used to disappointment.

If you make a mistake, or generate a result you did not intend, own it. Accept responsibility and ask what you can do to fix it. When you accept responsibility for your thoughts, emotions, actions, and their consequences, you are in control, you have the power, not Polly.

When you accept responsibility for your results, you can let others be responsible for their results. When you choose not to blame others, you can also refuse to accept blame. Trace back the results to the actions that created them to understand who is responsible. If your actions created part of the results accept responsibility for your actions but not for the actions of others that contributed to the result. Focus on correcting the result instead of making someone wrong. If nothing can be done, accept and learn from the result and, most importantly, move on.

You have the power to create whatever you want in your life. When you take responsibility for the results of your thoughts, emotions and actions, you are putting yourself in good hands, your own. Now the only thing standing in your way is Polly and you are capable of beating her and winning the game.

Desire

Emotion is like rocket fuel to the creation process. The greater your desire, the quicker you will manifest whatever it is you want. In fact, I encourage you to avoid using the word want when you are thinking or talking about a result you choose to manifest in your life.

Want is often used in reference to things we really don't expect to get. You hear or see something you'd like to have and wistfully say "I want that", with no real sense of commitment to creating it in your life. Want is used more like wish. It's like a small child wandering up and down the aisles of a toy store saying "I want this. I want that" to almost everything they see. You know, and I know, they're not going to get it.

Instead, think about the result as if you already have it. Picture it and build a feeling of desire around that image. When you desire something you crave it strongly and need to manifest it into your life. Wrapping desire around your thoughts will give a turbo boost to your efforts.

Focus

When you focus on something you engage the conscious mind. This is necessary to the manifestation process. Results are created by thoughts, emotions and actions. You've been operating on autopilot, letting Polly control your thoughts, emotions and actions and generate your results. Focusing on the results you desire supports you; having the thoughts and emotions to take action will generate those results. Remember, action is a requirement for change.

Commitment

While you are focused on generating the results you desire, Polly is going to be throwing up a variety of defensive maneuvers to defeat you. She is going to be planting all kinds of disempowering and limiting thoughts in your mind. Thoughts like "I can't do this", "It's too hard" and "I'm not good enough", designed to drain your desire and get you to quit.

Getting fully committed to the results means you refuse to accept anything less than those results. You commit to doing whatever it takes in order to generate those results. Commitment is about dedication and devotion to the results you are playing for.

One of the results I play for is a good quality of life, both now and in the future. I know that daily, consistent exercise supports that goal. My challenge is that I hate to exercise. I don't enjoy it and I have lots of programmatic excuses that run through my mind and leave me completely unmotivated to take action. I also know that motivation often does not precede action, it is a result of action. So it's my commitment that gets me out of bed in the morning and starts me walking. At some point my muscles loosen up and the endorphins kick in and then I feel motivated.

Affirmations.

Affirmations are short, positive statements you can use to reprogram your subconscious. A lot of the input used to create your associations and beliefs was disempowering and limiting. That input wasn't filtered and your mind wasn't developed enough to use reason and logic to figure out if it was valid. So it went directly into your subconscious and created disempowering association and beliefs, otherwise known as programs. Polly doesn't care if the programs she runs are empowering or disempowering, supportive or limiting. So those disempowering and limiting associations and beliefs are creating results you don't want in your life. You can use affirmations to reprogram disempowering and limiting associations and beliefs into empowering and supportive ones. I will discuss this further in the next chapter.

Goals.

Another way to help manifest what you desire is to write it down. When you write down something you desire it becomes a goal. Written, specific goals will cause the Universe to support you in manifesting what you desire. I will explain how to set goals and how they work in the chapter *How to Get What You Really, Really Want.*

Time

There are two beliefs about time that will support you in playing and winning the game against Polly.

The first belief is that the only time that exists is now. The moment of now is the only time in which your thoughts, emotions and actions can take place and generate a result. Yesterday and tomorrow don't exist in the moment of now. You can't do something yesterday or tomorrow in the moment of now. When you are thinking about the past or the future you are squandering your moment of now. You are wasting your opportunity to create a result by not being present in the moment. Being present in the moment means your thoughts, emotions and actions are focused around what is happening now.

You're not in the moment if your thoughts are about the past or future. Polly puts those thoughts in your head to control you. Thinking of the past often generates remorse over lost opportunities and what you could have done. Thinking about the future often generates fear over imagined results you don't want.

You can't do anything about the past in the moment of now. However, your thoughts, emotions and actions in the moment of now will create your future results. When Polly puts thoughts of the past or the future in your mind she prevents you from being present and taking action in the moment to create a result you desire. This creates more of the same results, which is what Polly wants. Polly wins, you lose.

The second belief about time that will support you is that there is no magic bullet or overnight success. If you examine your life you will see that this is true. It took you years to be able to walk and talk. It took years to learn all the things you now know and to be able to do all that you can do. Malcolm Gladwell, in his book "The Outliers", attributes becoming successful or an expert in any field as a result of practicing or working in your field for ten thousand hours. People who excel spend years honing their knowledge and skills. Success, getting what you want, is a result of consistent and sustained effort. As I've been telling you, repetition is the mother of skill.

You are bombarded by promises of immediate results and instant gratification. That's one of the basic tenets of marketing.

Just one application and your hair will look silky and shiny.
Your teeth will be noticeably whiter in only one week.
Lose thirty pounds in thirty days.

Do you know why advertisers make those promises? Because they work. Even though you know better, Polly gets you to believe the lie. Why does she do that? Because when you don't get immediate results or instant gratification, she can convince you to give up, to quit, it won't work, your efforts are doomed to result in failure. Then you go back to doing what you've been doing, which is what Polly wants. Polly wins, you lose.

See, Polly is always playing the game and she is a master at it.

I find the way Jeff Olsen talks about time, in his book "The Slight Edge", to be quite helpful and supportive. Draw a horizontal line on a piece of paper. This is your baseline. Time runs from left to right, now to the future. Above the line are decisions that support the results you're playing for. Decisions that don't support your desired results go below the line.

Every decision you make goes above or below the line based on whether it supports your results. If you're playing to be healthy, eating a salad goes above the line while eating a fast food burger and fries goes below the line. Neither decision, by itself, generates the result. If you eat a salad it doesn't make you healthy, nor does eating a burger and fries make you unhealthy in the moment of now. However, over time, your decisions compound to create a result. Choosing to eat foods that do not support good health can result in being overweight, having diabetes or a heart attack. Eating healthy can support the result of being healthy and free from sickness and disease.

Let me give you an example. Weight loss and gain is a very complex subject. For this example, I'm going to simplify it. At its most basic, weight gain and loss is a result of calories consumed versus calories burned. If you eat 1500 calories in a day and you burn 1500 calories, you will neither gain or lose weight, your weight will remain constant.

Now, let's add to this caloric balance one fun size candy bar each day. Pick whichever one you like, they tend to average 100 calories. That's a small imbalance, only 100 excess calories per day. Will you notice anything on day 1 or day 2? Nope. In fact, it will take 35 days before you gain a pound. That's based on one pound of fat being equal to 3500 calories.

Now one pound doesn't seem like a lot. Heck, your weight can fluctuate a pound or two during the course of a day. If you keep this up for a year, however, you will have amassed 36,500 extra calories. Divide that by 3500 calories in a pound and you've gained 10.4 pounds of fat. Chances are good you'll notice that in how you look and how your clothes fit.

That's the slight edge working against you. It was easy to make the decision that did not support your health goal and eat that candy bar each day. No big difference initially, you were just slightly below the line. By the end of a year you were on a definite downward course.

It doesn't stop there. What thoughts are you having after putting on that weight?

"I'm fat." "I'm disgusting." "I have no willpower." "I can't help myself".

And while she's putting those thoughts in your head, Polly is solidifying her position of power and control and making you weaker.

It took you one year to gain the weight. It's crazy to think you can take it off in a week or two. Polly knows this. Polly wants you to "fail" because then she can whisper in your ear "See? I knew I couldn't do it. I'm a failure. It's impossible. No sense in trying." Then Polly gets to keep control and generate your results. She is such a bitch.

So how do you generate a different result? Tell Polly to shut up and then do the math. If you can create a 500 calorie a day deficit, through eating healthy and exercise, you can lose one pound in a week. 500 calories times 7 days equals 3500 calories, or one pound. With focused and repetitive action you can lose the 10 pounds in 10 weeks. It's not going to happen overnight or in a week or two. But, through consistent action and supportive choices, you can lose the weight in two and a half months which is a lot less than the year it took to put it on. This is a realistic and healthy way to lose weight. It only works if you can ignore Polly's jibber-jabber and move beyond your programmatic thoughts.

There you go, those are the basic skills you can practice to support you in winning the game against Polly.

Chapter Seven

How To Be Happy

I was visiting my cousin who had just gotten an X-Box and had a first-person shooter game on it. I'm not a gamer, but I was interested in seeing how video games had progressed since the days of Pong, so I asked him to play the game so I could observe. Actually, the game was "Hitman" and what I said was "I want to see you kill somebody." Before he could begin to play the game he had to select a mission and get outfitted. There was about twenty minutes of prep work before he actually started to play the game and could kill someone to satisfy my bloodlust.

That's what the previous chapters were in the game you're playing against Polly. Now you know:
- how awesome the Real and Authentic You is;
- that you're engaged in playing a game against your programming to create all that you desire;
- how the game is played;
- how your opponent plays the game;
- the skills to develop to support you in winning the game.
- So, now you're ready to start playing.

On the cover of this book I promised to tell you how to be happy. I am now ready to deliver on that promise. All that you have to do to be happy is to:

Think happy thoughts.

Congratulations, you are now in the game. What thoughts is Polly putting in your head right now?

"What a load of crap."
"It can't be that easy."
"What does that mean?"
"How do I do that?"
"I can't do that."
"Are you joking me?"
"I already knew that, what a rip off."
"What do I do when I'm sad?"

Those and any similar thoughts are coming from your programming. They're not real. Here's what is real.

You can put any thought you choose into your mind. Choose to think about a parent, child, friend, pet, the Statue of Liberty or the Eiffel Tower and you can create a picture in your head. Your ability to think what you choose to think is real.

Your emotions are caused by your thoughts. You can't get angry without thinking about something that makes you angry, feel sad without thinking about something that makes you sad, or happy without thinking of something that makes you happy. That's real.

So if you want to be happy, think thoughts that make you happy in this moment and you will be happy. Every time you control your thoughts you are choosing to take back control of your life from Polly. Regardless of the thoughts Polly is putting in your mind, you can choose to reach for the thought that makes you feel best in the moment.

Yes, it really is that simple. Why would you think otherwise? You were born with the ability to control your thoughts and create what you desire. You did it as a baby and as a small child without any effort whatsoever. You're still creating, it's just not You that's creating your life these days, it's Polly.

You get to choose the emotion you experience in this moment. Why choose being miserable, or unhappy, or frustrated or any other emotion you don't enjoy? Where do your emotions come from? They're a result of your thoughts. Put happy thoughts in your mind and you'll be happy. The emotions you don't want to experience are also coming from your thoughts. Who is putting those thoughts in your mind? If you're not doing it consciously, then Polly is. Choose to think of something that makes you happy.

Really commit to playing the game. When you're feeling an emotion you don't enjoy, pay attention to what you are thinking about in that moment. Are you thinking about the future? What you need to do later today, who you've got to call tomorrow, taking the kids somewhere after school, a meeting with your boss? None of that is real, it doesn't exist in this moment and you can't do anything about it in this moment. Try to do something tomorrow, now. You can't do it. Are you thinking about the past? Something that happened that made you feel embarrassed, or angry, or upset? That isn't real either. None of it exists in this moment. So let all of those thoughts go. None of them support you being happy in this moment.

What could you think about instead? The vacation you have planned, places you want to visit, people you love, people who love you, a time in your life when you felt happy, a time you felt loved. If you think about feeling happy or loved how do you think those thoughts will make you feel? Happy and loved, of course! All I ever have to do to change the way I feel is to think about my grandchildren. That always makes me happy.

You could also use this time to focus on your goals and affirmations. I'll tell you more about affirmations later in this chapter, and more about goals in the next chapter.

The more often you take control over your thoughts, the faster your ability will grow and the stronger your mental muscles will become.

Polly is the one who doesn't want you to realize how simple it is to be happy. When you choose your own thoughts, instead of letting her put programmatic thoughts into your head, she loses control. Polly doesn't like that and she will do whatever she can to regain control. She is going to throw all kinds of disempowering and limiting thoughts at you in an effort to get you to stop choosing your happy thought and think about what she wants you to think about instead. Picture a monkey throwing poop at you. Not a pretty sight.

This is the essence of controlling your thoughts. It happens in the moment because that's the only time that is real, the moment of now. Whatever you're feeling in this moment is a result of what you are thinking. Change your thoughts and you change your emotions.

As simple as this is, it is going to be a struggle. You're used to letting Polly put thoughts in your mind. So, when you choose to control your thoughts it's going to be uncomfortable. Polly is going to tell you it's too hard. She will distract you so that you stop holding the happy thoughts in your mind.

Notice when that happens. Be aware in the moment. Tell yourself, "There's Polly, showing up to control my thoughts and run my life. Not going to happen, Polly. I control my thoughts and my life." Then put the happy thoughts back into your mind. Every time you see Polly showing up, rinse and repeat.

The only time that's real is now. This is the only time in which you can do something. You can't do something yesterday or tomorrow. Whenever you do something you do it in this moment of now. Yesterday and tomorrow aren't real, they are thoughts you are having in the moment of now. Don't waste your current moment of now, the only time that is really yours, on thoughts of the past or the future.

That's one of the ways Polly controls you. She gets you to think about the past or the future, has you think that her perception is real, and then gets you mired in judgmental thoughts making you right and others wrong. If you pay attention to, and examine, your thoughts in the moment, you will see that Polly has you thinking about everything except those things you really desire.

Your mission, if You choose to accept it, is to take back control of your thoughts and focus them on creating what you want in life and being happy. The programmatic thoughts Polly puts in your head are a distraction. They are not going to move you closer to creating what you truly desire in your life.

There are many moments during the day when your conscious mind is focused on the task at hand. When your conscious mind is engaged in an activity that is directly related to generating the result you are playing for, your thoughts are empowered and supportive.

It's the other times, when your conscious mind is not focused on what you are doing in the moment, that Polly takes over and fills your mind with disempowering and limiting thoughts. The more often you are not focused and present in the moment of now, the more opportunities Polly has to control you. She will fill your mind with programmatic thoughts that make you feel bad and get you to do things that aren't supportive of what you want.

These are the moments to be aware of Polly and the thoughts she is putting in your mind. Stories where you think your perception is reality and make other people wrong and judge them, or blame other people or events outside of your control for the results in your life. Thoughts that you're not good enough, or you lack something, or your powerless. Thoughts that do nothing to support you getting more of what you want, having a better life or being happy.

Polly is always playing the game and she is used to winning because you didn't know there was a game. It's time for you to get in the game and start creating the results you desire in your life. Pay attention, be present in the moment and replace the programmatic thoughts Polly puts in your mind with empowering and supportive thoughts. "Uh, Mark, what thoughts are those? I get what you're saying but I'm not sure what thoughts to choose in those moments."

Great question! You can choose to think of an affirmation. An affirmation is a statement that reinforces an association or belief that is empowering and supportive.

You have a lot of disempowering and limiting associations and beliefs. Take a piece of paper and make a list of them. Typically, these are "I am" statements. "I am stupid." "I am not good at reading." "I am clumsy." Think about and write down everything you can think of that you are not good at, all your weaknesses, all the negative things people say about you. While you're doing this, tell yourself that these disempowering and limiting associations and beliefs are not real. You created them based on sensory input that was not filtered or validated, it was simply accepted.

These programmatic thoughts are in your way so it's time to get rid of them. What IS real is that you are awesome and amazing, you have unlimited potential and the ability to create anything you truly desire. So now you're going to look at each of the disempowering and limiting beliefs and associations and write down the opposite. Instead of "I am stupid" write "I am extremely intelligent." "I am not good at reading" becomes "I love to read." "I am clumsy" becomes "I am graceful."

While you're doing this Polly will put thoughts in your mind like "No, you're not", and "That's not true" and "If I'm extremely intelligent why did I get such bad grades in school?". When she shows up you get to say "Hey, Polly, SHUT UP!" None of those thoughts are real. In fact, disempowering beliefs often become self-fulfilling prophecies. You believe you're stupid so you do stupid things. When asked why you did something stupid you reply "Because I'm stupid." If you believed you were intelligent, you might stop and think before you did something, and then choose a course of action that would generate a different, supportive result.

Bottom line, you're looking to create different results in your life than the ones you are currently experiencing. To achieve that, you must do something different than what you have been. Insanity is doing the same thing over and over, expecting different results. To do something different, you must think different thoughts. Different thoughts generate different actions, which create different results.

To become someone that has different thoughts you must replace the limiting and diempowering associations and beliefs with ones that are empowering and supportive. To do that you will employ the same techniques that created your current associations and beliefs.

If you have a belief that you are stupid, you didn't create that belief because someone said once that you are stupid. That's not enough reinforcement to create such a disempowering belief. That message was repeated over and over until, finally, your subconscious mind created that belief.

Repetition is the mother of skill. That's a double-edged blade that can cut both ways.

Another way that associations and beliefs are reinforced is through emotion. Strong emotion can quickly create a strong association or belief.

As a young child, you saw a hot burner on the stove and wanted to touch it. You were curious and it intrigued you. Your parents knew what would happen if you touched it so they told you "Hot!" and "No!" and pulled your hand away so you wouldn't burn yourself. But you really wanted to touch the burner. Eventually you managed to touch it and instantly regretted it. You felt an incredible amount of pain and immediately created a strong association and never touched a hot burner again. Well, at least not on purpose.

So, you are going to use repetition and emotion to reinforce your new, empowering belief or association. Pick one of the statements you wrote, like "I am extremely intelligent". Think it, in your mind, over and over, and over again. "I am extremely intelligent. I am extremely intelligent. I am extremely intelligent. I am extremely intelligent. I am extremely intelligent. I am extremely intelligent. I am extremely intelligent. I am extremely intelligent. I am extremely intelligent. I am extremely intelligent."

Do you think this is silly or stupid? Guess where that thought is coming from? Hello, Polly. It's a simple thing you can do that will support you in having everything you desire. It uses the same process that created the programmatic crap that Polly sticks in your mind all day long. It's silly and stupid to NOT do it.

You can repeat that in your mind over and over while you shower, shave, brush your teeth, get dressed, eat breakfast, drive or walk to work or school, or any other time during the course of the day when your conscious mind doesn't have to be focused on what you're doing.

Ready to kick it up a notch? Say it out loud. Even better, say it out loud while looking in the mirror and smiling at yourself and feeling TOTALLY AWESOME! The stronger the emotion the more powerful the reinforcement.

You might be wondering, "Really, Mark? Can repeating a simple statement over and over really change my life?" Yes, it really can.

Here's how it works. Until now, when Polly has put the thought "I'm so stupid" in your mind you haven't been paying attention. It has generated other programmatic thoughts and feelings resulting in you feeling anxious or angry or upset. Now that you know about programming, the next time Polly puts that thought in your head you'll recognize what she's doing. Instead of going down the rabbit hole after that disempowering thought, you'll think about your affirmation and tell yourself "I am extremely intelligent" one, or two, or a dozen times, remembering that repetition is the mother of skill. Replacing the programmatic thought with your affirmation will make you feel proud and powerful and happy. The more you repeat your affirmation, the greater your awareness of the programmatic thought, and the quicker you will replace it with your affirmation. After a while it will happen almost immediately and then, one day, you'll realize you don't even have the old programmatic thought at all anymore.

"So what, Mark? What good does that do me?"

That one disempowering thought does not live by itself inside your mind. "I'm stupid" comes with "I can't do that" and "I'm useless" and "I'm worthless" and a whole bunch of other limiting beliefs. These thoughts make you feel hopeless, powerless fearful and other disempowering emotions. How do you deal with what is happening in the moment of now when you are thinking and feeling that way? What actions do you take and what results do you create? You create the kind of life you have now, one in which you wish you had more, that your life was better and wondering how to be happy. You don't create a life of unlimited potential, filled with all that you desire.

You're not going to have to repeat the same affirmation for the rest of your life. You only have to repeat it until thinking it becomes a habit that no longer needs reinforcement. That time will vary based on how often you repeat the affirmation and how much emotion you put into it. The time will also vary based on how strong a hold the disempowering association or belief is and how often it comes up in your life. The more you repeat the affirmation with emotion, and the more frequently you are able to challenge Polly and replace the programmatic thought, the faster the programmatic thought will disappear.

You don't have to limit your work with affirmations to one at a time. You can work on multiple affirmations during the course of the day. I would keep it between three and five so you don't have too many to focus on and are able to do enough repetition each day to adequately reinforcement the affirmation. You can write your affirmations on post it notes and index cards to keep you focused on repeating them. Post it notes can be stuck on mirrors, your dresser, the fridge, the console in your car, anywhere you're likely to notice them and have a few moments to repeat them. Index cards can go in your pocket, briefcase or purse as the same kind of reminder.

Playing the game means being aware of the thoughts in your mind in the moment. Not the moments when you are consciously engaged in something, but in the moments when your mind is "wandering". I put that in quotes because your mind is not really "wandering", it's being filled with programmatic thoughts by Polly. Pay attention to those thoughts and replace any disempowering or limiting thoughts with empowering and supportive ones, like affirmations. Disempowering thoughts include stories about other people or events that happened in the past, stories about future events, made up conversations, judgmental thoughts and blame.

When you interrupt your programmatic thoughts, emotions and actions, and choose a different thought to create different emotions and actions that will generate a different result, you win the game and Polly loses.

Chapter Eight

How to Get What You Really, Really Want

To get what you really, really want, you follow a simple process known as goal setting. You were born with the ability to set and reach goals. When you were young you used it all the time, without any conscious thought or effort.

When you were born all you could do is eat, sleep, poop and cry. As you developed, you started wanting to do more. You wanted to gain motor coordination, control over your actions, so you observed others and practiced until you could grab things and hold them and manipulate them. Then you set a goal to turn over and you achieved that. Next came sitting up, then crawling. Every time you achieved a goal you set a new one and you accomplished them all, right up to the first big ones, walking and talking.

Once you turned control of your life over to Polly, she put the kibosh on setting and reaching goals. Polly is all about running the same programs over and over and getting the same results. She has no interest in goals. She doesn't want anything to change, she wants to keep churning out the same results, just like that CNC machine and the chair legs.

Chances are good you still get some of what you want. Polly is not running things all the time. There are periods when you're in conscious control of your life and creating some results. Other times, your programming may be in alignment with creating what you desire. This chapter is designed to support you in consciously creating anything you desire.

Whether you realize it or not, you are always working towards a goal. If it's not a goal that you have set and desire, then you are working on someone else's goal. That may be your boss, spouse or parent, or Polly's goal of keeping things exactly how they are.

Before we look at the creation process, let's look at what you really, really want.

If you were to create a list of the things you really, really want, what would be on it? Would it be filled with material items, money, a house, a car, clothes, exotic vacations and things like that? I get it, I want a lot of those things too. Do you know why you want those things?

I'm pretty sure you don't want money because you're interested in collecting pieces of paper with pictures of dead notables on them. "Mark, now you're just being silly." Yes, yes I am. So why do you want money? For all the stuff it can buy, of course. Money will buy you the house, car, clothes, vacation and anything else you want.

Yes, that's true, money will buy you all of those things. That doesn't explain why you want those things. A twenty year old Toyota will get you from point A to point B. Is that the car you want? "Mark, you're still being kind of a doofus. Of course that's not what I want. I want a high performance Italian sports car." Or a high end truck, or SUV, or luxury sedan. Something sleek and smooth and sexy and powerful.

Got it. So why do you want what you want? What do you get out of a high performance Italian sports car or current model luxury sedan that you won't get out of a twenty year old Toyota? You won't get the rush, the feeling of power, of being sexy, of fun, of being successful, that the car you want will provide you. You won't get the same feelings.

That's why you want what you want. Everything you want, you want for the same reason, how it will make you feel. What you really want is to feel good. Since there is no good or bad without judgment, which is programmatic, let's say you want to feel the emotions that bring you pleasure, the emotions you enjoy.

It's important to recognize this when you start to focus on what you really want and how Polly is behind the scenes manipulating you.

What do these people have in common? Michael Jackson, Whitney Houston, Heath Ledger, Anna Nicole Smith, Chris Farley, Kurt Cobain, Margeaux Hemingway, River Phoenix, John Belushi, Elvis Presley and Marilyn Monroe? They all achieved a level of success and fame that most people aspire to, and died tragically due to alcohol, drugs or both. Some of them died accidentally and some committed suicide. Their fame and financial success did not bring them the feelings they were looking for, so they used alcohol and drugs to change and manipulate their emotional state. People self-medicate all the time to control their emotions and "feel good". It works, sort of. It can suppress the thoughts creating the feelings temporarily and to some extent. Eventually the effects wear off and you're left with the thoughts that are making you "feel bad".

Where do those thoughts come from? Polly, of course. It's your programming putting those thoughts in your head to control you. Your emotions are a result of your thoughts. It's an inside job, as my yoga instructor says. Nothing external, like using alcohol and drugs, can create a different result. The only way to win that game is to take control of your thoughts and choose thoughts that support the feelings you enjoy. That's something only you can do for yourself and no one can take those results away from you. You win, Polly loses.

It's important you understand that nothing outside of yourself is going to impact how you feel. Your emotions are a result of your thoughts. Happiness and all of those other pleasurable emotions you desire come from within. You can achieve all of the success, fame and fortune you desire and still not feel what you want to feel if Polly is directly controlling your thoughts and indirectly controlling your emotions.

That being said, let's look at how you can be, do and have whatever you desire.

You have the ability to create anything you desire through your thoughts. Goals are used to expedite the creative process. There are simple guidelines to follow when setting goals.

- Write down your goals.
- Goals are written as if already achieved. I am, I have, etcetera.
- The goal states what you want, not what you don't want. Rather than a goal to stop smoking set a goal to live smoke free; a goal to be sober rather than to stop drinking or stop doing drugs.

Here's a basic goal.

I have a new car.

It's written as if you've already achieved it and it states what you want. Here's another example of a goal.

December, 1, 2017. I am so happy and grateful
now that I have a 2018 Lexus LS 460 F Sport with a
Satin Cashmere Metallic exterior, a Flaxen leather with
Shimamoku Espresso trim interior, and the Executive-Class
Seating Package.

Yeah, I'm not sure what that interior is either, I saw it on the Lexus website. Regardless, there are three factors that make this second goal more powerful and have greater impact.

- Be clear, specific and detailed in describing your goal.
- Include a target date by when you will obtain your goal.
- Invoke the benefits of emotion

Here's why you write down your goals and why that second goal example is more effective and powerful. You write down a goal so that you can read it over and over again. Repetition is the mother of skill. The more you read and focus on your goal, the more you drive it into the subconscious. The conscious mind is limited in what it can focus on. The subconscious mind, however, is powerful and amazing and has an enormous capacity to work on things behind the scenes. By driving the goal into the subconscious mind, we engage the subconscious into using all of its power and abilities. Did you ever go to sleep thinking about a problem you had and found that you had a solution when you woke up? Your subconscious was working on finding a solution while you slept and it was there for you when you woke up. How awesome is that? That's the power you tap in to when you engage the subconscious mind using goals.

You write the goal as if it's already achieved because the subconscious mind cannot differentiate between real and imagined. It's the conscious mind that reasons, analyzes and filters. That worked against you when you were young and exposed to all sorts of disempowering and limiting sensory input. Your conscious mind couldn't analyze, reason and filter out the crap so it went straight into your subconscious and created associations and beliefs that were disempowering and limiting. Now you can use your subconscious mind to support you in getting what you really, really want. When the conscious mind tells the subconscious that you already have whatever it is you want, the subconscious mind believes it and works on manifesting the result the conscious mind has envisioned.

Your goal states what you want because the subconscious processes results. Stop smoking is a non-result, it's about not doing something. The subconscious doesn't get that, it wants to generate a result, so it will ignore the stop and focus on the action, smoking. This will not support the result you desire. Write your goals so they will support result you desire, in this case living smoke free.

Fuzzy goals create fuzzy results. Be specific, detailed and clear so that you will get the results you are playing for. This higher degree of focus will also make it more real to the subconscious, getting it to work harder and faster at manifesting the result.

You put a date on your goal to give it a sense of urgency. With no date it becomes a someday goal, and someday usually winds up being never. A date supports you in creating a time line to support your plan. If your goal is to lose ten pounds in ten weeks you can create a plan to lose one pound a week.

There are other things you can do to turbo boost your efforts and create the results you desire even quicker.

The more you think about and focus on your goal, the faster it will manifest in your life. At a minimum, read and think about your goals twice a day, once when you wake up and once before you go to bed. Write your goal on an index card and carry it around with you and look at it whenever you can during the course of the day. Every time you read your goal, you increase the engagement of the subconscious in achieving the goal.

Read your goal out loud to engage the additional sense of hearing. Increasing the amount of sensory input will boost the impact on your subconscious.

Take it to the next level by visualizing your goal. Get a clear picture of what you want in your mind. The mind works in pictures, not words. Get a picture of the 2017 Lexus LS 460 F Sport with a Satin Cashmere Metallic exterior and a Flaxen leather with Shimamoku Espresso trim interior, and look at it while you read and think about your goal. Picture yourself driving it. The more real it is to the subconscious, the more effective it is in manifesting the goal.

Use emotion. The greater the emotion when reading and visualizing your goal the greater the impact on the subconscious. That is why you include being happy and grateful when you write down your goal. Feel the excitement and joy you have driving your Lexus. Imagine yourself behind the wheel, driving down the street while people stop and watch you go by. Experience how that feels as you hold that picture in your mind. Emotion is a very effective way to turbo charge the creation process.

Emotion is also the reason I use the words "really, really want" and "all that you desire" when talking about your goals. The emotion of desire is like rocket fuel to the goal achieving process. Your subconscious is not going to get that fired up by something you wistfully want, or wish you could have. A deep desire is like a fire burning in your belly that won't be quenched until you manifest whatever it is you desire.

When you set a goal you define a result you are playing for which creates a new game. Who are you playing against? Polly, of course, and she is going to try and derail this process. She'll start by putting thoughts in your head when you start making a list of what you really, really want. She'll put thoughts like "Oh no, that's crazy, I can't have that", or "How can I possibly get that? There's no sense in even thinking about it", or "I can't do what it takes to have that." She'll continue as you work through this process. "It's too hard", "The price is too high", or again, "I can't", which is one of her favorites.

Bull-dookey! Of course you can! You were born with the ability to create. There's nothing hard about it. Remember, hard is not real, it's a perception. You've been creating and manifesting all your life, you can't help doing it and you're still doing it. The difference is that you've been creating unintentionally and by chance. Now you're going to create consciously, with focus and determination on what you desire and choose to create.

If I've made it sound like all you have to do is write down and think about your goal and then it will suddenly appear in your life, I apologize. That's not all there is to it. Granting wishes is what a genie does and, by the way, genies aren't real. The next step in the process is to create a plan.

This is another opportunity for Polly to show up. "How do I create a plan?" "I don't know what to do." "It's too hard. " And Polly's favorite, "I can't".

Yes, you can. You don't need to create a comprehensive, detailed plan. There is a gap between you and your goal. You must fill that gap with action steps. Remember, nothing will change until you take action. Fill in the gap with things you can do to move you closer to your goal. All it takes is one or two action steps to get you started.

As you think about and focus on your goals, repeating them because repetition is the mother of skill, visualizing them while feeling the emotions achieving them will bring, and taking action to start the process of manifesting them in your life, an interesting thing will happen. The Universe will start to send thoughts, people and circumstances to support you in achieving your goal. This is why you don't need to have a detailed, comprehensive plan in place before you start. You have no idea of what is going to show up in your life once you attract the power of the Universe to help you.

This may sound a little like "woo woo", but I assure you, it's not. I'm going to give you a brief explanation to help you understand how you harness the power of the Universe when you create, and how you can focus that power through setting and working towards goals.

When you study personal development, you will repeatedly come across references to the Universal Laws. These Universal Laws are not the same as the physical laws of the Universe. The Universal Laws, not sure why but they are usually capitalized, are considered to be timeless truths. I don't know where or with whom they originated, even after asking "the Google". They are supported by a large amount of data acquired through observation and experimentation over a very long period of time. However, you won't find this data in scientific journals or textbooks as they are more philosophical and metaphysical in nature.

You know about the physical laws of the Universe, like gravity. It's what keeps you attached to the earth and prevents you from floating off into outer space. You also know that if you choose to ignore gravity there could be dire consequences. There are plenty of documented cases of that on YouTube and America's Funniest Home Videos. So you know that you are subject to the natural laws of the Universe whether or not you understand or believe in them.

You're also familiar with many types of energy, like heat, light, sound, radio, and electricity, all of which are subject to physical laws. One of the Universal Laws that applies to energy is the Law of Vibration. The Law of Vibration states that all energy vibrates. This is also something you know if you think about it. Heat comes from molecules vibrating, the faster they vibrate the more heat they generate. Light is measured in wavelengths, a wave being movement between two points, or vibration. Different wavelengths, or vibrations, result in different colors of light. Outside of the visible spectrum of light there is infrared, ultraviolet and microwaves, all vibrating at a different frequency. Change the vibration of sound and you change the pitch. When you switch radio stations you're tuning your radio to a different frequency, or rate of vibration. So the Law of Vibration fits into what you already know to be true.

Now consider that, over time, what we know about the Universe changes. Throughout the course of human history, scientists have told us "This is truth", and then discovered that they were wrong and told us "Forget what we said before, THIS is the new truth". The earth is flat, the earth is round; the sun revolves around the earth, the earth revolves around the sun.

I get it, it's all part of the scientific process. They theorize and experiment and study and learn. Sometimes they develop new technology that can examine things that couldn't be examined before. As a result, our understanding of the Universe increases a little bit more.

When I was young, I was taught in school that the Universe is made up of matter and energy. Matter was all of the physical stuff I could see and touch. Everything else was energy. So everything in the Universe was either matter or energy. Thanks to Quantum Physics, we now know that the Universe is actually made up of energy. What we view as matter, or physical particles, are really particles of energy vibrating at a rate to appear solid. If you look close enough at everything in the Universe that seems like matter, you will see that it is actually made up of vibrating particles of quantum energy that only appear to be solid matter.

Before I bore you to tears, I'm telling you this to explain how another of the Universal Laws works. The Law of Attraction says that energy is attracted to energy that is vibrating at the same frequency. In other words, when it comes to energy, like attracts like.

So, what are your thoughts made of? If you didn't immediately answer energy, you must have fallen asleep during the previous paragraphs. When you set, focus on and visualize a goal, with emotion, you are sending energy out into the Universe. That energy is vibrating in alignment with what you desire. Those vibrations attract thoughts, people and circumstances to support you in achieving your goal.

That makes it scientific "woo woo".

By the way, it works the other way as well. If you focus on what you don't want, you're sending that energy into the Universe and attracting what you don't want. Did you ever notice how often you get exactly what you don't want? Polly creates that result by putting thoughts of what you don't want into your mind. That's why it's so important to focus only on what you want.

Another way goals support you in getting what you desire is through motivation. When you are motivated, you tend to take action. So motivation moves you towards your goals.

What about those times when you aren't motivated, when you don't feel like taking action? Motivation is an emotion, which is a result of your thoughts. If you're not feeling motivated, it's because of the programmatic thoughts Polly is putting in your mind. Polly is good at playing the game and keeping you from taking action. She does that because she knows that action can create motivation. One of my commitments to my health goal is to wake up early and walk every morning. I don't like waking up early and walking. I have absolutely no motivation to do that, ever.

I am, however, committed to my results. So I use discipline and commitment to get me up and walking every morning. An interesting thing happens about 20 minutes into my 30 minute walk. I start to feel really good. The endorphins are kicking in and my muscles have loosened up and I'm feeling happy and suddenly I am motivated to walk! But none of that occurred before I started walking.

While discipline and commitment are supportive, they're not always enough to get you going. What do you do when you don't feel like doing anything? You read your goals, rinse and repeat. It takes very little energy to pick up the index card, piece of paper or notebook on which you've written your goals. Regardless of the thoughts Polly is putting in your head and how you feel, you can probably get yourself to do that. The first time you read them you might scan the words quickly and they'll have very little impact. That's why you read them again, rinse and repeat. After a couple of readings you start to pay attention to the words. After all, these goals are things you desire, things you really, really want. As you keep reading your goals your mind will start to connect with the words. You'll start to visualize the goal and what achieving it will feel like. Before you know it, BAM, instant motivation. OK, so it wasn't instantaneous, but you will feel motivated, I guarantee it.

At this point you might be motivated to work on one of your action steps. Even if you don't, you're putting thought and emotional vibration into the Universe to put the Law of Attraction to work for yourself. Sounds like a win - win to me.

As our discussion of How to Get What You Really, Really Want draws to a close, there's one final item to look at.

TANSTAAFL

That stands for There Ain't No Such Thing As A Free Lunch. Just like a nice dinner at a fine restaurant, there's a price to be paid.

Ah, I can hear Polly now, putting all those programmatic thoughts in your brain. "I knew it, there's a catch, there's always a catch." "Told you, too good to be true." "Whatever the price is I can't pay it." "Just another bait and switch."

Yay, another opportunity to move beyond your programmatic thoughts! I told you, Polly is always going to be there, trying to subvert your efforts. Instead of letting her run the show, choose a different thought. "Of course there's a price, I get that. I know there's no such thing as a free lunch. What exactly is that price, Mark?"

The price is one you can easily pay. Remember, you are creating all the time. Every result in your life right now you created. So you've been paying the price. The only difference is now you're going to consciously create and pay the price.

The price consists of paying attention to your thoughts, controlling them so you move beyond programmatic behavior, choosing the thoughts that will support you, setting your goals, reading and visualizing your goals to leverage the Law of Attraction, and taking action steps to manifest the result you desire.

Here's Polly, once again. "I don't have time for that." "My life is too busy." "That sounds like a lot of work." "Waaa, waaa, waaaa." That's what Polly really sounds like. I encourage you to start hearing her that way.

All of those programmatic thoughts Polly is putting in your head are more bull dookey. Everyone has the same number of hours in a day, the same number of moments of now with which they can create. You might have to turn off the TV, leave work on time instead of leaving late, let your kids amuse themselves instead of you amusing them, go to bed a little later or wake up a little earlier.

It doesn't matter how little money or education or skills you have. None of that can be used to pay the price for happiness and to get what you really, really want. Everyone has plenty of the currency that's required; focused thoughts, emotions and actions, energy, and time.

Knowing all this, if you choose not to pay the price, at least you won't have to wonder why you don't have the life you desire.

Let's talk about your goal list. A goal is anything you want to be, do or have. It's easy to come up with things you want, material goals, and things you want to do, like exotic vacations. I encourage you to think about and set goals in a variety of areas. The key here is balance. You don't want to achieve a bunch of material goals only to find out that they do not provide the feelings you truly desire and leave you feeling unfulfilled. Here are some other areas to think about and include when creating your goal list.

Personal Development
Becoming the person you choose to be; how you choose to show up in the world; how to get more of what you want; how to be happy.

Financial
Income level, how much you earn per month or year; becoming debt free; your net worth; the ability to buy the things you really, really want.

Family / Love
Relationship with your spouse or partner; date nights; your children; your extended family.

Health
What you choose to eat; walking; working out; yoga.

Spiritual
Connecting to a higher power; believing in something larger than yourself; organized religion.

Career
What you want to do with your life; getting a new job; getting a promotion; starting a business.

Social

Getting together with friends; start or join a book club; playing sports; other group activities.

Remember, when writing your goal list **anything goes!** There is no idea too crazy or goal too big. You can create anything you desire in your life. If it exists, you can have it. If it doesn't, you can create it. If someone else has done something, you can too. If no one else has done it, you can be the first. There's always a first, why can't it be you? There's no real reason it can't be you, but you can be sure that Polly is going to show up and tell you why you can't have or do whatever it is you desire. Don't let her limit you. Don't worry about how you're going to get or do whatever it is you desire. When you engage the power of the Universe to support you, **ANYTHING** is possible!

When setting goals, it is supportive to have both big and small goals. Big goals make you stretch and reach and grow as a person while achieving smaller goals along the way helps to keep you motivated.

I can guarantee that Polly is going to keep showing up during this process. That's fantastic, it gives you lots of opportunities to confront Polly. You can't get rid of programming, it's how the mind works. You can be aware of Polly when she shows up. You can confront her and choose your thoughts, emotions and actions in the moment, rather than letting her run the same programs that disempower and limit you.

As you review your goal list, you might think to yourself "Wow, that's too many things to work on at once." Congratulations, you are correct! That's one of the main reasons New Year's resolutions fail, trying to change too many things at once. Another reason is the lack of a plan. And Polly is always right there, putting disempowering and limiting thoughts in your mind, so nothing changes and she gets to run your life and create the same results over and over.

Once you have written out your goal list, the next step is to prioritize and organize your goals. Some goals are more important to you than others. Starting your own business might have a higher priority than getting together with friends once a week. Some goals must be accomplished before you can move on to another goal. You have to complete the goal of writing the book before you can become a published author. Some goals may have a timetable of their own. The photography class you want to take may only be offered two months from now. Big goals will require more time and effort than smaller goals.

I think three goals is the most you can be actively working on, and only one of those can be a big goal. A big goal would be to get sober, be smoke free, or recognize your defensive behavior and choose to move beyond the programmatic response.

Small goals would include having a date night once a week, walking for a half hour five times a week, or putting away all electronic devices at the dinner table and conversing.

Small goals require little planning and are easy to set up and accomplish. If your goal is to have a date night once a week, the plan might include getting your partner to agree, committing to the same night every week or sitting down with your calendar and picking a specific night each week for the next three months, and creating a list of date ideas. After that, all you have to do is be aware of when it's date night and go out on a date.

"Mark, that sounds good but our lives are really busy. What happens if it's date night and we can't go on a date?"

Good question. I get it, life happens sometimes. Let's look at three concepts, commitment, integrity and accountability.

When you set a goal for date night and create the plan, both parties get to commit to it. A commitment is a pledge or promise that you bind and obligate yourself to. When you commit, you promise to do everything in your power to honor your commitment.

When I speak of integrity I am not talking about character and principles or morals and ethics. I am talking about integrity as in being whole. A ship's hull has integrity as long as it keeps water out. If you put a hole in the hull so it leaks, then it no longer has integrity.

So when you commit to something and you are not able to honor that commitment, for whatever reason, you are out of integrity with your commitment. In other words, your commitment is not whole, you did not fulfill the promise you made with your commitment. Own it, acknowledge your lack of integrity regarding your commitment and recommit. Acknowledgment of your lack of integrity to the person you committed to is called accountability. Accountability is supportive of having integrity to your commitments. It's also part of accepting responsibility.

I have an accountability partner that I text every night regarding my integrity to my health goal commitments. It's very easy for Polly to put rationalizations and excuses to ease my mind when I am out of integrity. After a couple of days I hardly even think about it. When I'm the only one that knows of my commitments and integrity to those commitments, it's easy to blow them off. When I have to text someone daily, there is pain involved in admitting to being out of integrity. If I'm out of integrity for two or three days I am seriously motivated to show up with integrity in regards to my commitment.

If you find yourself consistently being out of integrity with one of your commitments, I invite you to reexamine your goal and see if it's something you truly desire. If it's not, cross it off your list and work on a different goal. If it is something you truly desire, work on your description of the goal and why you want it. Clarity and desire will support your integrity.

If it's to be, it's up to me.

You, and no one else, are responsible for the results you create in your life. Setting and working towards goals is how to get what you really, really want.

Chapter Nine

Preventing The Negative Influence
Of Other People

Are you ready to play the game with other people? Are you confused because I told you that you don't play the game against other people? If you're not confused, congratulations, you're paying attention. If you are confused, I encourage you to pay closer attention. As the saying goes, the devil is in the details.

You don't play the game **against** other people, but you do play the game **with** other people. You always play the game **against** Polly. However, when you interact **with** other people, which you probably do all day long, the way you show up with these people is based on whether you're winning or losing the game **against** Polly.

You know you only have direct control over one thing in the Universe, your thoughts. In this chapter I will show you how, by changing your thoughts, emotions and actions to move beyond your programmatic behavior, you can win the game against Polly and get other people to treat you differently. As you read through this chapter, pay attention to the thoughts Polly is putting in your mind. I guarantee that the things I tell you in this chapter will have Polly up in arms and coming at you with her WMDs.

How much of the results you have in your life do you blame on other people? Do you think your life would be better if your parents, kids, husband, wife, boyfriend, girlfriend, boss, employees or coworkers were different? Let me give you a hint, NO, IT WOULDN'T!

That's Polly putting those thoughts in your head. Remember, blame is Polly's game. Blaming others for the results in your life is programmatic. Blaming others is one of the reasons why you are getting the results you are currently experiencing. Blame is disempowering and limiting. Blame takes away your power to create all that you desire. That suits Polly, she doesn't want any different results. Having you feel powerless to change your life fits right into her plan.

If you believe your success and happiness are dependent on other people, you have two chances to get what you want, slim and none. Taking responsibility for your thoughts, emotions, actions and the results they generate enables you to use the power you already have to create whatever you desire. Regardless of what it is that you want to have in your life, there's only one way for you to get it:

If it's to be it's up to me.

Accept responsibility, play the game against Polly, win the game and move beyond the programmatic thoughts, emotions and behaviors that currently limit you, and no one will be able to stop you from being, doing and having everything you desire.

"That's easy for you to say, Mark, but my _____ treats me horribly and makes my life a living hell." Fill in the blank with boss, husband, wife or whomever it is you blame for the crappy results in your life. That's blame, that comes from Polly, and it makes perfect sense that Polly tries to blame others for your results. After all, Polly, in the guise of the programmatic thoughts, emotions and behaviors that are running your life, is the one generating your results. Polly accepts no responsibility, she is master of The Blame Game.

Here's why you get treated the way you get treated by others.

People don't treat you the way they treat you because of
who they are,
they treat you the way they treat you because of
who you are.

Have you ever known someone that almost everyone liked? You know, one of those rare individuals that seem to make friends with everyone they encounter. On the other hand, have you known someone that almost everyone disliked? A person who seemed to have no redeeming qualities whatsoever. You liked the first person but not the second. Why? Did you change who you were between meeting the person you liked and the person you disliked? Of course not, it was the person you met and how they appeared and behaved that determined your response to them.

In other words, it's how you show up that determines how others treat you. More specifically, it's who you show up as, what program is running, that determines how others treat you. When you show up as a victim, people treat you like a victim. When you show up like a control freak, people treat you like a control freak. When you show up as the Real You, open, honest, vulnerable and accepting, people have the space to be who they are and they will like you for that.

If you want other people to treat you differently, it's not going to happen by getting them to change who they are. You have no control over other people. Like you, they are programmed and their programming is going to keep on generating the same thoughts, emotions and actions to create the same results. To be treated differently, **you** must show up differently. If people are used to you showing up as a victim and you show up as a confident person, they won't be able to run the same programmatic responses they ran when you showed up as a victim. They will be forced to consciously reinterpret who you are and how to deal with you. Let me give you an example that most people can relate to.

The 6 Most Powerful Words - I Admit I Made A Mistake

Those words were printed at the top of a poster entitled "A Short Course In Human Relations" on the wall in the barber shop I frequented when I was growing up. I thought they were profound then and I'm even more convinced of it decades later. Everyone makes mistakes. We're all human, and humans are not perfect, humans make mistakes. Mistakes are a part of learning. There's an expression, you learn more from your mistakes. That's because the emotions associated with making a mistake drive it forcefully into your subconscious. You don't really learn more from your mistakes, it's that your memory of the lesson is stronger and more firmly fixed in your mind.

Polly, in the form of the control program, is always on the lookout for mistakes. The control program is all about blame and judgment, making itself right and others wrong. You see this a lot in bosses, parents and individuals that have a supervisory position. Being in charge really brings out the control program. When you make a mistake, it's a wonderful opportunity for the other person's control program to exercise power, enthusiastically emphasizing how wrong you are. They will tend to ask questions like "What were you thinking?" and "How could you be so stupid?" over and over, while droning on and on about the cost of the mistake. All of this is designed by their programming to make you feel terrible and themselves feel powerful.

When you're being berated, what are you thinking and how do you feel? You're thinking that you are stupid and not good enough. You're feeling embarrassed, ashamed and humiliated. You might also be thinking that it's only a mistake, that everyone makes mistakes and you can fix things if this person would stop yelling at you and let you get back to work. Those thoughts might make you angry and result in your having a few choice words in your head which you'd love to share but never will. At least not with them. You might share your thoughts later with a coworker or friend as your program works on making the person who yelled at you wrong and yourself right.

Chances are good you've experienced or seen this situation recur many times with the same boss, parent or authority figure. Wouldn't it be great if they would change and stop acting like that? Yes, it would, and that's not going to happen. You can't change them, so that's not a solution. The way to create a different result is for you to show up differently. Here's what that looks like.

When you are first confronted about the mistake, accept responsibility for the mistake and apologize for it. You are responsible for the consequences of your thoughts and actions. If something you said, did or didn't do resulted in the mistake, own it. Your programming is going to try and place blame on someone or something else. Move beyond that programmatic response by accepting responsibility. Accepting responsibility is one of your weapons and this is how and when you wield it. Tell the other person, "I made a mistake".

When you accept responsibility you are going to confuse the control program that the other person is running. Remember, programs run the same way every time. The same thoughts, emotions and actions are generated every time a program runs. It's kind of like a choreographed dance with each person knowing and executing their part. Their control program expects you to blame someone else, that's how the blame game is played. Then it gets to prove the mistake is your fault, making it right and you wrong, so it feels powerful and in control and you feel like crap. By accepting responsibility you derail that whole process, forcing it to move on to the next moves in the dance.

The next move is for their control program to repeat how wrong you are and berate you for what you did. This is the "What were you thinking?", "How could you?" and "Are you stupid?" phase. Both your program and their program know that there is no answer to these questions other than the answer that was already given, you made a mistake. It's just an opportunity for their control program to feel powerful and you to feel like crap; for their program to be right and you wrong. Are you seeing a pattern here? You have been programed to be silent here because any sort of answer gives fuel to their control program to continue berating you. Better to be quiet and let the fire burn out. Of course, being quiet also triggers the control program to continue to rant and rave, so it appears you really can't win in this situation.

Here's how you extricate yourself from these dance moves. At the first opportunity, acknowledge how the other person is feeling and how you feel. Repeat that you understand you made a mistake. If you can, identify the cause of the error; you missed something, weren't paying close attention, made the wrong decision, misread or misheard. Let them know that you understand the cost of the mistake and ask how you can fix it. For example,

"I get that you are very upset over the mistake I made. I'm upset as well. I take pride in the work I do and my goal is to do the best job possible every time. I did not meet that goal this time and we're going to have to do this over, costing the company time and money. I am truly sorry I made this mistake. What can I do to fix things?"

Their control program will definitely be confused. This is not how the dance is supposed to go. Once it's been derailed like this, there's a strong possibility that their program will move on. They may have a final comment to make but the dance will be over. A really strong control program may try to trigger you and get your programming back in the dance. If, rather than moving on, they continue to berate you or engage you in any other way simply say,

"I get that I made a mistake and you're upset. I've admitted my mistake, apologized for it, and asked what I can do to fix it. What else would you like me to do?"

99% of the time this will end it. After all, what else can you do but what you've done? You can't go back in the past and undo the mistake. The other person's program knows that there is nothing else you can do and will recognize that continuing to run the program after you've accepted responsibility, apologized and asked how you can fix it will reverse the power, making it wrong and you right. The program can't have that so it will turn control over to another program, maybe know-it-all so the other person can tell you what to do and be right and have power once again.

If you're dealing with the 1% that just can't let go, rinse and repeat. Don't engage, don't make excuses, don't do anything that their program expects. Simply say again,

"I get that I made a mistake and you're upset. I've admitted my mistake, apologized for it, and asked what I can do to fix it. What else would you like me to do?"

Anything else will trigger the same programmatic response you're looking to end. Your program may want to make them wrong for continuing the dance. Don't do it! They have the high ground because, after all, you did make a mistake. Acknowledge, apologize and move on is the result you're playing for.

This may sound simple, but to generate this result you will first have to move beyond your own programmatic responses. Your program will be making you wrong and trying to get you to feel bad. You might be thinking "I can't believe I did that. How could I be so stupid? Who can I blame for this? What am I going to say?" Recognize those thoughts as being programmatic and replace them. "I made a mistake. I'm human and humans make mistakes. I will take responsibility for my mistake, apologize and do whatever I can to fix it. I will learn from this so I can avoid future mistakes."

If you're able to replace your programmatic thoughts and emotions with empowering ones you will be able to show up differently in your interactions with other people. When you show up differently, people are forced to deal with you differently. That's how you impact their behavior.

I started with this specific example to show you that it is possible to change other people's behavior by changing how you show up because I know it works. Control is one of my core programs and I run it hard. For years I was that a-hole employer who ran the very program I just described. This was many years ago, early on in my journey of personal development, before I learned about programming. I ran that scenario thousands of times and it never changed, the results were always the same. That's how programming works.

It's important to understand that the same programs run in all areas of your life. So my control program was generating the same situation at home. Polly would run the same program when my wife and kids made a mistake. And it always generated the same result.

Once I learned about programming, I was able to see what was happening and choose to move beyond the programmatic behavior to generate a different result. Now when my wife makes a mistake, I choose different thoughts, creating different emotions and behavior. However, Polly never goes away and sometimes, when my control program gets triggered by someone making a mistake, I don't move beyond the programmatic response and the old program runs. It still works and it still generates the same result. That's not the result I want to generate so I've had conversations with my wife about this program and the results I want to generate. I have asked her to support me by doing exactly what I described in the preceding paragraphs. Every time she does that my control program recognizes that continuing would make me an a-hole and it stops. It works every single time, and not because of all my work in personal development. When my programs run I am as much a slave to them as anyone else. It works because it makes the program wrong and Polly can't let that happen so she moves on.

What I've described here applies to any interaction with another person, regardless of the relationship. When it comes to personal interactions, people run the program that complements the other person's program. When somebody comes up to you and acts aggressively, how do you react? A victim will be intimidated and submissive. I am an aggressive person and will be aggressive right back to them. Your reaction will be based on your programming, and it will be in response to how the other person showed up. Other people are going to react or respond to you based on how you show up. By that, I mean what program you are running when you interact with them.

Zig Ziglar made an interesting observation regarding the words react and respond. When it comes to medication, react indicates an adverse effect while respond means the medication is having the desired effect. People tend to react when they encounter disempowering and limiting programs like anger and blame. They respond to empowering and supportive programs like happiness and acceptance. Paying attention to how people appear when you interact with them can give you a good indication of how you're showing up. If they're reacting to you, examine your thoughts, emotions and actions and change your thoughts so you show up differently in that moment. Then you can completely change your interaction and win the game against Polly by generating the results you are playing for.

What do you think would happen if, for one whole day, every time you encountered someone you put a big smile on your face? I'll bet that almost everyone would smile back at you. My wife and I walk in our neighborhood at 6:00 AM every weekday morning. The same people drive past us every day on their way to work. One day I decided to smile and wave at every car that passed us. No surprise, people smiled and waved back. I kept doing that, day after day. Now when we walk, a lot of those people are smiling and waving at me first. I impacted their behavior by changing my thoughts, emotions and actions. Not only that, I feel happy when they smile and wave at me and I'll bet at least some of them feel the same way.

How Do You Feel About That?

Everything you desire in life you want because of how it will make you feel. Your feelings come from the only thing in the world you control, your thoughts. Any feelings you desire you can generate yourself by thinking the thoughts that will create those feelings. It's really a perfect, closed loop system. A toddler can have just as much fun playing with the box the toy came in as they can playing with the toy.

Polly doesn't want that, she wants to control your thoughts, feelings and actions. So she convinced you that other people were in control of your emotions.

"He makes me so mad."
"She hurt my feelings"
"You're stressing me out"

Do you get how crazy that is? No one can make you feel anything. You can feel hurt but you can't hurt feelings. Stress is an emotion created by your thoughts like all of your emotions. What's really happening is that Polly is generating the thoughts that create the emotions as a reaction to what someone said or did. As you know, Polly is just the name I give to the collection of programs you run, the associations and beliefs you've created. So it's really you generating the thoughts that create the emotions. I say it's Polly so you'll understand that you're doing it without conscious intent.

What Polly is doing is using blame to give away your power to others so that she can maintain power and control over you. She is such a bitch.

Your interactions with other people are no different than any other sensory data your mind processes. They say and do something, you interpret what they say and do, you say and do something, and they interpret that. What's real is that they said and did something and that you said and did something. Everything else is perception, an interpretation of what happened.

Who's doing the interpreting? Most of the time it's Polly. Unless you're consciously focused on choosing an interpretation in that moment, it's your associations and beliefs that are interpreting what the other person said and did.

Why not choose an interpretation that makes you feel happy, or content, or loved? It's as simple as deciding on an interpretation that empowers or supports you instead of letting Polly choose the interpretation for you.

What thoughts is Polly putting in your mind right now? Is she giving you all of the reasons why you can't do that? That's more programmatic crap she's shoveling at you. Remember:

Your perception is not reality.

Your perception is simply your interpretation of reality. That is an extremely important distinction when it comes to getting what you want from other people. It's difficult to move beyond your programs and your programmatic responses if you're stuck in the belief that your perception is reality. That belief creates the illusion of right and wrong. This leads to judgment and giving Polly the power to run her programs and continue to generate the same results you supposedly no longer want in your life.

When you let go of the belief that your perception is reality, you can be open and honest and accepting of other people. When you do that, you create space for them to show up differently.

A person's programming will react or respond to the way in which you treat them. Dale Carnegie, in his book "How To Win Friends and Influence People", talks about giving a dog a good name. The concept is that people will live up to, or down to, the reputation you give them. So give them a good reputation to live up to. By treating people in a way that encourages and supports the result you're playing for, they become your teammate, someone who's on your side, supporting you in creating the result you desire.

Do you think that other people's words and actions are responsible for what you think, how you feel and the subsequent actions you take? THAT'S NOT REAL.

Words have no power on their own, they're simply words. The word asshole describes a part of the human anatomy. It is also used to describe an individual ehibiting less than flattering behavior. If we're talking anatomy, saying asshole may make me snicker because I'm a guy, but it probably won't generate much else in the way of thoughts, emotions or behavior. If I prank you and you call me an asshole I'll just laugh knowing I pulled one over on you. If you beep your horn at me and call me an asshole while driving I'm going to yell back and flip you off. Maybe run you off the road because I have serious road rage.

Same word, three different scenarios, all with different thoughts, emotions and behavior. It's not the word that has power, it's how you interpret the word in that moment that creates your perception of reality and, possibly, gives it power.

Think about the "N" word. As a white male, if someone calls me that it's not going to have any impact. I may wonder if they know what the word means, or if they're color blind, but I certainly won't get all hot and bothered by it. By the same token, if I walk into Harlem and start throwing that word around there's a very good chance I'll seriously offend some people. Yet I've heard African-Americans use that word with each other without taking offense. Does the reaction and result come from the word? Of course not, it comes from the interpretation of those hearing the word. That interpretation is influenced by who is using the word and their perception of how it is being used.

You have the ability to choose the meaning of what you see and hear. When Polly is in charge it's all about judgment and right and wrong and power and control. She is going to interpret what you see and hear in a way to support your programming, creating the same results you've been getting.

Here's another example for you. A mother is always a mother, no matter how old their kids are, and my Mom is no exception. When I would visit my Mom, she would tell me to turn on a light when I was reading, or to wear a jacket when I went outside, or any of the other thousand things mothers say to their children in an effort to take care of them. That's what a Mom does.

This would trigger my programming. It would generate thoughts like "I'm a grown man, I'm not stupid, I know when to wear a coat or turn on a light, I can take care of myself, I don't need her telling me what to do." Thoughts control emotions and these thoughts resulted in my program getting angry. Really angry, over the top angry, stupid angry. Polly would make my Mom very wrong for saying those things to me.

What was real in this situation? Real was that my Mom spoke words. My perception of those words was that she thought I was incompetent, incapable of taking care of myself and she was trying to control me. Her perception was that she was doing her job, taking care of me. The result of this difference in perception was that I would get angry and yell at my Mom to make her wrong and make her feel bad, to try and control her future behavior. Which, of course,never worked. She continued to say those things in an attempt to take care of me because that's how she is programmed.

Once I became aware of what was happening, I decided to create a different result. When she told me to turn on a light or put on my coat, or gave me any other motherly advice, I decided to interpret that as her way of saying "I love you, Mark." I changed my perception of her communication, what her words meant to me. "Put on your coat" became "I love you" in my mind which made me feel good. Now when she gives me some motherly advice I laugh and tell her "I love you too, Mom." I have created a completely different result simply by changing my interpretation of what she said. I let go of the programmatic interpretation Polly created and my Authentic You replaced it with an empowering interpretation.

A friend was telling me about her conversations with her mother. Her perception was that her mother was critical of her and said mean and hurtful things to her. I shared with her this story about my Mom and her motherly advice. I told her how I changed the whole experience by choosing to interpret my mother's words in an empowering manner. I suggested that when her mother said mean and hurtful things, she could choose to interpret it as the only way her mother had of saying "I love you".

When I said that, she looked at me and said, "Oh no, I can't do that." "Why not?", I asked. "Because she really means it." Was her reply. Obviously, she didn't understand the point I was trying to make. Which is to be expected. Unless you've been given the background and basis in the preceding chapters, your programming won't allow you to hear the message.

You, however, now understand how the mind works and you know about programming. You can see that it's not what people say, or what they mean, or how they look, or what they do that creates meaning for you. It's how you interpret the communication that determines what it means to you. In any moment you have the choice of how to interpret the sensory input you receive. Choose to interpret it in a way that makes you feel good.

Here's something you can do the next time you're in a situation where Polly is interpreting someone's communication in a disempowering way. If your interpretation, your thoughts, about that person's verbal and nonverbal communication is that they are angry, or disdainful, or disgusted by you, you're going to feel an emotion you don't enjoy. You might feel anger, shame, guilt, sadness or some other distressing emotion. In that moment, tell the other person that you choose to interpret what they're saying as meaning they love you and that you love them as well.

They will become apoplectic trying to convince you that they are really angry or disdainful or disgusted by you. Just smile and tell them "Nope, I choose to interpret what you're saying as meaning you love me." The more they try and convince you they mean something else, you simply tell them "I love you too!" Then simply walk away. Their head might explode and you will feel great because you completely changed that interaction by choosing a different interpretation.

That's what I did when I chose to interpret my Mom's advice as meaning "I love you" instead of "You're too stupid to turn on a light". I chose to interpret her words in a way that made me feel warm and loved. That's what my friend could have chosen to do when her Mom said whatever she said to her. Since Polly is running her life, her programming made up a story to make her Mom wrong and her right. That program will keep running until she decides to change it.

I'm sure Polly is generating thoughts to make me wrong. "That sounds great, Mark, but life is not all flowers and rainbows and unicorns. I wasn't born rich, I have to work for a living. My job sucks, so my life sucks."

Why do you choose to look at it that way? Why do you choose that interpretation? Of course it's actually not you interpreting it that way, it's Polly. So why do you let Polly interpret it that way for you?

This is really the simple, basic concept behind getting more of what you want, having a better life and being happy. In every moment, you get to choose what your sensory input means. Choose the thought and interpretation that makes you happy and supports creating the result you want. Which means you have to be aware of the result you want.

Of course, that can only happen if you choose to be present in the moment. Then you can stop Polly from running her programs that are designed to keep you stuck right where you are, getting the same crappy results you don't want.

I get that work is necessary to provide the basic requirements of life; food, clothing, shelter and security. People have always had to spend time doing that. In the old days time was spent hunting, gathering, finding water and shelter. Now we work to make money to pay for those things. We need the basics to survive, but they don't really fulfill us. Beyond that we want friends and social relationships, love and intimate relationships, self-esteem and a feeling of accomplishment, and to utilize our potential in helping others and creating. You can choose to focus on those things that you want and simply view work as a means to an end.

"It's not that easy. My life is hard. Things are complicated. Blah, blah blah".

That's just Polly talking trash. It is whatever you believe it is. Are you going to choose your interpretation or let Polly interpret for you? She's the one that created the life you currently have. To get more of what you want, have a better life, and be happy, you are going to have to take back control of your life from Polly.

It really is that simple. When Polly is filling your mind with all of her programmatic thoughts and emotions, the thoughts and emotions that generate the actions that create the same result you don't want, all you have to do is stop and ask yourself "What result am I playing for? What result will empower and support me in getting what I want?"

The challenge is going to be Polly. She doesn't want to give up control. She is going to bombard you with her programmatic thoughts. When you first decide to move beyond your programming and choose the thoughts, emotions and actions that support the result you're playing for, it will be a bit of a struggle. That's because you've been conditioned to let Polly have her way.

Conditioned behavior is another way to look at what I call programming. You may be familiar with conditioned behavior The most famous example is Pavlov's dogs. When food was placed before them they would salivate. While they were salivating over the food a bell was rung. The dogs associated the ringing bell with getting fed. Over time they started to salivate when they heard the bell, even if there was no food.

That's right, Polly has conditioned you like you were one of Pavlov's dogs. Certain things that people say or do act as a trigger, like the ringing bell. When they happen Polly puts thoughts in your head that generate emotions and actions that create the same results every time.

Conditioned behavior, programs, are like ruts. When you were born you were like a grassy field that no one has ever driven on before. The first time you drive across the field you are creating a trail. Initially it's faint, hard to see, like your associations when they are first formed. As you drive along the same path through the field, over and over again, the tires create ruts in the ground. This is the repetition that conditions your behavior, creating the program. Eventually the ruts become deep, hugging the tires and creating a smooth ride. Now your programs, the conditioned behaviors, have taken control. There's no thinking involved, you're just following the past of least resistance. To get your car out of this rut takes effort. There's going to be a few bumps. To move beyond your programming, to do something other than what you've conditioned yourself to do, is going to take effort and will be uncomfortable.

It's empowering to remember that you are the one who conditioned the behaviors. You created the associations and beliefs that created the programs. All it takes is some focused, conscious effort to reprogram yourself. You can't get rid of programming, your mind is always going to create and beliefs. You can recognize disempowering and limiting programs and replace them with ones that empower and support you in getting the results you are playing for.

I've told you that people treat you the way they do because of how you show up, and that you can generate a different result by showing up differently. Another good example of this can be found in that much dreaded interaction, a call to customer service.

I am in customer service conversations quite often. I have been providing computer support to small and medium sized businesses for over 30 years. I work diligently to provide exceptional service and excellent support. I know that if I don't, my customers are going to call someone else next time. So I tend to expect the same level of service from companies and people who provide service to me.

That's the programmatic set up. For me, providing good customer service is critical because I'm in business for myself. If people stop using my services, I don't make any money and can't pay my bills and I'm in big trouble. On the other hand, most of the customer service conversations I have are with employees of corporations. For them it's just a job and a paycheck. They are not vested in the quality of service the same way I am. Cable and cellular providers have millions of customers and make tens or hundreds of millions of dollars every month. My perception is that I don't have any leverage to get the result I'm playing for.

When I contact customer service, like you, it's because I've got a problem. Typically, the problem has upset me or made me angry. If I show up as angry Mark, I have a 99.99% failure rate when it comes to getting the result I'm playing for. Angry Mark speaks harshly and uses blame and is generally unpleasant to the poor customer service representative, who did not create the issue I am having. This tends to make the customer service rep extremely unhelpful.

On the other hand, when I show up as friendly Mark, explain my problem, accept responsibility if appropriate, request help, complement the person helping me, and show gratitude, I have a 99.99% success rate at getting the result I'm playing for. I can even get a little angry if I follow it up with an explanation that I'm not angry with the person I'm speaking to, I'm angry over the situation, and I apologize for being angry and really appreciate their help and support.

I've gotten my cellular carrier to send me a signal booster for free, the cable company to replace the underground cable to my house and install conduit to protect it, my timeshare company to extend my points for two months saving me hundreds of dollars, a multitude of late charges and fees waved, and so forth. You get the idea.

In these situations, the result I'm playing for is to get the customer service rep to give me something. When I show up empowered, positive and friendly, I enroll them in helping me. That supports getting the result I'm playing for. When I show up angry and disempowered, I am often looking for satisfaction. I want to make them wrong and myself right, and I want them to admit it. Nobody likes being made wrong, so they are not enrolled in helping me and I usually don't get the result I'm playing for.

This is how Polly controls and subverts your interactions with others to prevent you from creating the results you desire. She puts judgmental thoughts in your head, like her interpretation of right and wrong, to distract you from showing up in a way that supports getting the result you're playing for.

If you're playing for getting something for free, or a fee waived, those results are real. The result is more money in your pocket. Admit a mistake, ask for help, be nice and appreciative. Those thoughts, emotions and actions will support getting your desired result. Polly's interpretations and attempts to place blame or gain power and control will not get you what you're playing for.

It would be wonderful if I could give you an example for every interaction you might have with another person for the rest of your life. But, I can't. Instead, I can tell you what to watch for and give you some tools to support you in winning the game.

Pay attention to your interactions with others. Polly wants you to believe that your perception is reality. Then she can get you to make up stories, be judgmental and play the blame game. Is that what you're doing and how you're showing up? Watch how other people interact with each other. Can you see them doing the same thing?

If someone says or acts in a way that your programming interprets as negative, how do you react or respond to them? You probably react in a like manner. Their programming will similarly interpret your words and actions, and they will react by making up stories, being judgmental and playing the blame game. You react, they react, and everyone's programmatic interpretation is reinforced. Polly wins, you both lose, and no one gets the result they were playing for except Polly.

When it comes to playing the game with other people, the key is to be open, honest and accepting. Regardless of how they show up, choose to accept them. Don't make up stories about them or judge them or blame them. Focus on the results. Use empowering and supportive language. Ask questions. When you show up this way, it creates space for them to show up differently.

To generate a different result, you must be present in the moment. Being open and accepting is going to be uncomfortable. Polly is going to make up stories and put thoughts into your mind to make the other person wrong. You must go into the moment prepared to accept them without stories or judgment regardless of how they show up. It is going to take practice. Repetition is the mother of skill. You will fall back into your programmatic behavior, losing that game. Remember, you get to play again, and again, and again. Interacting with other people is not going to go away. The more you practice, the more you play, the more you will win.

Chapter Ten

How To Get More, Better, Happy, Long Term

Do you think you're ready to start playing the game? Then you're not paying attention. The reality is you've **been** playing the game and you're **always** playing the game. Remember, the game is played against Polly. She is always there, in your head, feeding you thoughts to generate the programmatic responses that will keep creating the same results in your life that you've been getting. Now, you know about Polly, how she plays the game, and how to beat her,

CONGRATULATIONS!

You have just leveled up. That's a video game term used to indicate that a player has become proficient enough to go to the next level. The next level has a greater degree of difficulty and requires a greater level of skill. Reading this book has accomplished that for you.

So, now that you've leveled up, what's next? You've got all of this new information about how awesome you are and that you can create anything you desire. You've learned how your current results are being generated by your programming, and how to take back control of your life from Polly. You also know that knowledge isn't enough. In order to create different results, to get more of what you want, have a better life and be happy, you must take action. So, what do you do now? What's your first step?

Are you excited, anxious to get going? That's how I am when I learn something new and level up in the game. Start by taking a deep breath. This isn't a sprint, it's a marathon. There is no destination, it's a journey. The goal is to be present in the moment so you can enjoy your life. We all know the eventual destination and I, for one, am in no rush.

You get to play against Polly from the moment you wake up until you fall asleep at night. Getting more of what you want, having a better life and being happy occurs as you win the game more often. To win more often, you practice the skills I've described in this book. There's not really a first thing or any specific sequence to follow. At any moment you can recognize, confront, and change your programmatic thoughts.

Success, in the context of more, better and happy, is a natural result of winning the game more often. To win more often, you work on the basics every day. The basics are the skills that support you in getting the results you desire. Repetition is the mother of skill. As you work on the basics, you will be building your mental muscles, increasing your ability to beat Polly at her own game.

The Basics

Cultivate being aware. Be present in the moment. Everything happens in the moment of now. If you're not present in the moment, you can't recognize and change the programmatic thoughts to create different results. Being present in the moment is a habit. Two of the best tools for building awareness, being present in the moment and creating new habits are post-it notes and index cards.

Until you have trained yourself to be present in the moment, developed the habit so you don't have to think about it, you need to remind yourself. Write down a reminder on post-it notes and stick them in places where you're going to see them throughout the course of the day. You can stick them on your bathroom mirror, dresser or dresser mirror, kitchen counter, refrigerator, car dashboard, desk and any place else where you'll see and read your reminder over the course of the day. You can do the same thing with an index card and put that in your pocket or purse, or tape it up like the post-it note.

The specific message doesn't really matter as long as it gets you to focus on being present in the moment and paying attention to your thoughts, emotions and actions. You can write down messages like:

What am I thinking of right now?
How am I feeling?
What thoughts are creating my emotions?
Am I present in this moment or are my thoughts somewhere else?
What could I do right now to empower or support myself?

When you read and think about your note you will be present in the moment. The more often you are present in the moment, the quicker you will develop the habit. Eventually you will not need the reminders because you will have conditioned yourself to live in the moment.

As you focus on your thoughts in the moment, notice if you're thinking about what you want or what you don't want. Your thoughts send out vibrational energy that attract support for what you're thinking about. If you think about what you don't want, you're attracting results you don't want in to your life. Always focus on the results you desire. You can use post-it notes and index cards to remind yourself by writing messages like:

What result am I playing for?

Do my thoughts in this moment support the result I'm playing for?
I always focus on what I want.

Polly is an expert at filling your mind with disempowering and limiting thoughts. Stories about the past, stories about other people, judgmental thoughts, thoughts of what you don't want, fearful thoughts of what the future holds, reasons why you can't, why it's someone else's fault, how other people are responsible for your life sucking, and on and on and on. She fills your mind with all of these thoughts that prevent you from focusing on and creating the results you do want. That's why you don't get more of what you want, why you don't have a better life, and why you're not happy.

When you are present in the moment, you will realize that a significant portion of your day does not require conscious thought. Polly is using that time to fill your mind with all of her programmatic crap. It's no wonder she's been winning the game. Choose to use that time to focus on your affirmations and goals.

Create affirmations and goals. Review the chapter "Playing the Game" for support in creating affirmations and the chapter "How To Get What You Really, Really Want" for setting goals. Once you have developed them you can write them on post-it notes and index cards to support you in focusing on them when your mind is not consciously occupied in the moment.

Recognize your programmatic thoughts. This requires being present in the moment and choosing to be aware of the thoughts in your conscious mind. If you're not intentionally putting thoughts into your conscious mind, Polly is. Programmatic thoughts are easily identifiable. They include:

Thinking that your perception is reality and that other people should accept it as such.

Making up stories about other people, believing you understand their intentions or the meaning of their thoughts and actions.

Being judgmental, including using judgmental words to describe people or situations. Right, wrong, good, bad, easy, hard, etc., are perceptions or interpretations. They vary from person to person and are not real.

Playing the blame game. Accept responsibility for your thoughts, emotions and actions and their consequences. Don't blame other others and don't let others blame you. They are also responsible for their thoughts, emotions and actions and the consequences.

Any thought that is disempowering or limiting. Thoughts like "I can't", "I'm stupid" and "I'm a loser". The Real and Authentic You is amazing and able to create anything You desire.

Change your programmatic thoughts in the moment they occur. This is the skill that will have the most impact on your life. It is the reason you must be present in the moment. You can't change your programmatic thoughts after they have triggered and run the programmatic response. It's too late, the program has run and Polly has won. Game over, play again. Your programmatic thoughts are generating your emotions and actions and creating the results you are experiencing. Every time you replace a programmatic thought with an empowered or supportive thought, you will generate emotions and actions that create the results you desire. This is where the game is won or lost.

Practice acceptance. Acceptance comes from the Real and Authentic You, not from Polly. Accept other people for who they are. Accept that everyone has their own perceptions and interpretations and that yours are no more or less valid than anyone else's. Accept that things are the way they are and that wishing they were different won't change them. Acceptance is the opposite of programmatic thinking. As you practice and strengthen your level of acceptance, you weaken the hold your programming has on you.

Choose the thought that makes you feel best in the moment. There's that "in the moment" concept again. Your thoughts are not real, they're perceptions. If Polly is filling your mind with programmatic thoughts, all you have to do is choose to think of something else. Remember, your thoughts are the only thing in the Universe you have direct control over. Not feeling happy? Choose to think about something that makes you feel happy. Thinking about what you don't want? Choose to think about the results you do want. Thinking any sort of disempowering or limiting thought? Choose to think about your affirmations, goals or how awesome and amazing you are.

When dealing with other people, choose to interpret their words and actions in a way that supports you getting the result you want. If their words and actions are designed to make you angry, choose to show up differently. When you do, you confuse their program giving you the opportunity to create a different result. Alternately, choose the interpretation that makes you feel best. If someone says something mean, choose to interpret it as their way of saying "I like you!" Polly is going to play hard to prevent this. She wants to control the stories to further her own agenda.

The reality is that you never really know someone else's meaning or intention. Only they know that. You cannot see into their heart and their mind. Even when they clearly state something, they may not truly mean it. People say things they don't mean all the time.

Not necessarily because they are duplicitous, sometimes their goal is to spare someone's feelings, or avoid confrontation, or any one of a million other reasons. Meanings of words may differ between people. Interpretation of non-verbal communication, like facial expressions and posture, can vary significantly. You know how easily communication can be misunderstood and misinterpreted.

So whatever thoughts you have in response to another person's words and actions are not real, they are an interpretation. Polly is the one telling you it's real so she can run her programs and win the game. Shut her down by choosing to interpret what other people say and do in a way that supports you.

Another way to weaken Polly and help yourself win the game is to move away from using programmatic words. Eliminate judgmental terms based on perception, like right and wrong, good and bad, easy and hard. Instead, use the terms empowering and supportive or disempowering and limiting. There words relate to the end result, not the person or situation. Instead of focusing on an interpretation, like good or bad and right or wrong, these words focus on whether you are getting closer to, or further away from, the result you desire.

Repetition. Have I mentioned that repetition is the mother of skill? Of course I have, I have repeated because it is the skill that will speed up the process and condition your behavior to support you getting more of what you want, having a better life, and being happy. Rinse and repeat. Do it again. And again, and again. It's easy to see how repetition supports improvement when you look at sports. Want to get better at shooting free throws in basketball? Shoot 100 every day. Want to get better, faster? Shoot 1,000 every day. Want to improve your forehand in tennis? Hit a forehand shot against a wall 100 times a day. Or 200, 500, or 1,000. The more you practice, the better you get.

This may not seem like enough to get more of what you want, have a better life and be happy. You might think that changing your life requires some big event, an "Aha!" moment, or some other momentous event. I get it, I used to think that as well. I would finish a book or an audio program, complete a course or go to a seminar and be looking for that magic bullet that would instantaneously change me and my life.

There is no overnight success. It doesn't work that way. It's practicing the basic skills, day after day, that creates the results you're playing for over time. Any person who has achieved any significant level of success in their field has done it that same way. Repetition is the mother of skill.

Forty years ago I read my first personal development book. I was in the Navy and stationed on Guam, far from home and feeling very alone. I felt I had incredible potential for more, the ability to make my life far better, but I had no idea how to tap into that potential. Worse, I was completely unaware of any resources that could support me. What I did have was a goal and a strong desire. That was enough to get the Universe to help me out. One day I came across the book "Looking Out For #1" by Robert J. Ringer. I don't remember if I saw it in a bookstore or someone gave it to me or I found it laying around the house where I lived. I don't even remember what the book was about, beyond the obvious message contained in the title. What I do remember is having an epiphany when I read the title. I got it, right away. I've got to look out for me because no one else is going to.

That was my first step on my journey of personal development. As I learned more, through reading, audio tapes and seminars, I decided that my purpose, my mission in life, was to help other people who wanted a better life and didn't know how to get it.

How has that worked out for me? Well, since leaving the Navy I have earned a living by providing computer support to small and medium sized businesses. Not exactly the result I was playing for.

I have nurtured that goal for forty years. It's a result I have played for again and again. I have played and Polly has beaten me time after time. Polly has used all of her tricks with great success. She has put disempowering and limiting thoughts like "I'm not good enough", "I can't do it", "It's too hard", "There's too much competition", "Who do I think I am?", in my head to undermine and sabotage that goal. She has confused my reality with her perception, made up stories, used judgment and blame very effectively.

Every time it was Game Over and I had lost, I knew I could Play Again. I truly believe that failure only occurs if I give up. As long as I continue to play I haven't failed, I just didn't get the result I was playing for. I was determined to reach that goal and now, at sixty years old, with the publishing of this book, I am generating a result I was playing for and won the game.

Here are a few stories that exemplify what is possible when a strong belief is coupled with desire. We've discussed beliefs, which are ideas you chose to accept as true without proof. They can be based on something seen, heard or misheard. They require no facts or truth to support them. Some beliefs are easily given up or modified. Other beliefs can be immensely powerful. Henry Ford understood the power of beliefs when he said:

"If you think you can do a thing or think you can't do a thing, you're right."

Henry Ford believed that thinking that something can be done is enough to bring about success. In 1928, Henry Ford ordered his engineers to start work on an eight-cylinder engine, the V8. Chevrolet had introduced a six-cylinder engine that was negatively impacting the sales of Ford automobiles. Rather than follow Chevrolet, Ford decided he would lead by delivering an innovative V8 engine. At that time, V8 engines were only used in luxury cars due to the manufacturing cost. Ford's vision was for a V8 that could be cast as a single piece and mass produced, making it affordable.

The challenge was that it could not be done with contemporary technology. After some initial research, Ford's engineers reported that fact to him. He told them he understood and directed them to go and build him a V8 engine cast in a single piece. You see, he understood the difference between fact and belief. More time and money were spent and again the engineers reported failure and that it could not be done. Ford was adamant that they continue until they succeed. The Ford Motor Company needed that V8 engine in order to compete with Chevrolet and they were going to create it for him.

Over the course of four years Henry Ford had four different teams of engineers working on different designs. Finally, in 1932, Ford introduced a low-priced car with a V8 engine to compete with Chevrolet's six-cylinder engine. That success was a direct result of Henry Ford's belief that it could be done, regardless of what the experts told him.

Polly may be putting a lot of programmatic thoughts in your head right now. Telling you stories like Henry Ford's success was due to some made up advantage he had over you. Being judgmental, convincing you her perception is reality, blaming others for the results in your life, doing whatever she can to make me wrong. I get it, that's what Polly does.

Let me tell you about some people of whom you may not have heard. First is Jennifer Bricker. This young lady was given up for adoption because she was born without legs. Her adoptive parents decided to raise her with no limitations and only one rule - never say the word can't. Jennifer, a girl with NO LEGS, became the top tumbling champion for the State of Illinois. She also played softball and basketball in high school. She moved to Hollywood where she lives independently, drives a specially made car, earns a living as a gymnast and has the goal of being a star. Did I mention she has NO LEGS?

Anthony Robles was born with only one leg. He started wrestling in eighth grade and as a freshman in high school he had a record of 5-8. In his sophomore year he was ranked sixth in Arizona, won the state wrestling championship in both his junior and senior year, and won a national championship as a senior. At Arizona State University he went on to become a three time PAC-10 Champion, a three time All American, and an NCAA National Champion.

Tim Harris was born in 1986 with Down syndrome. In his teens he started to dream of owning his own restaurant. In 2010 he opened Tim's Place, the first and only restaurant to be owned by a person with Down syndrome. Tim feeds more than hungry bellies, he feeds the soul. Everyone coming into his restaurant is greeted with a hug. He has given out more than 60,000 hugs to a variety of people including Stevie Wonder and President of the United States Barack Obama. He now has a successful speaking career inspiring people around the country.

These stories are incredible and illustrate the unlimited potential that lies within all of us, including you. Missing limbs, developmental delays and physical disabilities caused by a genetic disorder aren't enough to suppress that potential. That's the power of belief and desire. So tell Polly to shut up and don't listen to her programmatic reasons why you can't get what you want. Instead, get a clear picture of your goal, focus on it with a strong feeling of desire, believe that you can create it and take action until you manifest it. Henry Ford, Jennifer Bricker, Anthony Robles and Tim Harris did it, and so can you.

Chapter Eleven

Now What?

How do feel right now? Are you excited about all of this new information that's rolling around inside your brain? Can you see clearly your potential and believe in your ability to create everything you desire? I know that's how I am every time I finish a seminar, or an audio training, or a book. I've done that hundreds of times over the years.

Then Polly shows up. She's able to sabotage me with one simple question.

"Now what?"

Those two words strike at the core of my insecurities and disempowering beliefs. That's where Polly lives, where she's the strongest. I start to think "What do I do now? How do I get started? Who do I think I am? I can't possibly do it right. Besides, this is stupid. Everyone knows that this personal development crap doesn't work. Who am I kidding? I'm a failure. I don't have what it takes to be successful. No sense in even trying." Before I even get started it's Game Over.

In case you're like me, and you're feeling a bit overwhelmed by what you've learned, here's a simple 5 step plan for you to follow.

1. Take a deep breath and exhale slowly.
2. Tell Polly to "Shut Up!"
3. Write down one empowering thought.

4. Write down one goal.
5. Spend 10 minutes a day on something positive, motivational or empowering.

There is power in your breath. Deep breathing will help to calm you, making it easier to focus your attention.

Telling Polly to shut up makes you aware of her voice in your head. Awareness is the first step in replacing the programmatic thoughts with empowering thoughts.

 The key concept, the simple message at the core of everything I've told you is this - control your thoughts. Control your thoughts means choose the thought that's inside your mind, rather than letting Polly put all of her programmatic thoughts in there. Initially, your mental muscles are weak and atrophied because you haven't been using them. So, keep it simple. Write down one empowering thought that you can use as your go to thought. Put it on post-it notes where you'll see them. Write it on an index card and look at it often throughout the course of the day. Whenever you become aware of Polly, and the disempowering or limiting thought she's putting in your head, you'll replace it with your empowering thought. Here's an empowering thought you could choose.

"I am TOTALLY awesome!"

Every time you become aware of any programmatic thought in your head think to yourself "I am TOTALLY awesome!" again and again and again. As you repeat this you will start to feel awesome because your thoughts create your feelings. That's all there is to controlling your thoughts.

Your goals are the things you desire, what you want to create in your life, what you want to be, do or have. To manifest you need to put energy into your goal. That's why you write it down and read it, think about it, and visualize it as frequently as possible. Thinking about your goal is another thought you can choose when Polly shows up.

To get better at something you need to work on it, put energy into it and take action. Commit to spending at least 10 minutes a day on you. Reread this book or get some other personal development resource. Work on your goals or your affirmations, meditate, practice yoga or exercise. Do something that will support and empower you every single day.

As I said, I know from experience that it can be challenging to create different results in your life on your own. You may be all fired up now, after reading this book. Taking action, whether it's reading a book, listening to an audio program or attending a seminar, generates motivation. That creates a desire to take more action and generate new results. But Polly has been playing and winning this game for years. Polly is patient, sneaky, and she knows how to win. She will use time against you, continuing to put disempowering and limiting thoughts in your head to wear you down, so she can sneak back in and take over your life once again. On your own, it can be very challenging to develop the habits and build your skill set to the level where you can consistently win against Polly.

This is why every athlete has a coach, someone to support, encourage, and motivate them, and keep them focused on the results they desire. A coach can also provide training to help them develop the skills they need to succeed. Coaching has expanded beyond sports. You can now get performance coaching, career coaching, life coaching, business coaching, executive coaching, health coaching, nutritional coaching, and so on.

Being part of a community of likeminded people is another way to get support. This is why Alcoholics Anonymous and Weight Watchers are such effective and successful programs. In the forty years it has taken me to reach my current level of knowledge and skill, I achieved more, faster, when I had the support of people who shared my beliefs and goals. While this book is a result of those forty years of study and practice, it is not the culmination of my efforts. This book is a springboard, the first step in my goal of using what I have learned and who I have become to support people who want to be more, better and happy.

This is my mission for the next phase of my life:

To create a self-sustaining community that will support individuals choosing to take back control of their lives and create results that are in alignment with their goals.

In my mind, that's a big goal. How am I going to achieve that goal? I don't know yet. I do know how I'm going to start, which is all I need to know. I am going to present seminars and workshops locally to anyone interested in attending. I am going to utilize technology and the Internet to share my training and bring people together. There are so many ways available to do that today, even if people are geographically far apart. I will be utilizing webinars, email, conference calls, and blogs. I will ask questions to determine what type of support interests people. I will empower people to help each other. I will refine and expand my plan along the way. I will keep playing the game until I have reached my goal, that anyone seeking the support of a community will have access to it.

It all starts here, on my website.

http://morebetterhappy.com

That's it. Now it's time for you to take action. Go to my website, write down some goals or affirmations, or notice a programmatic thought and change it.

Control Your Thoughts

Control Your Life

Mark Coté is the president of Independent Computer Support, Inc., a privately owned company providing I.T. support to small and medium sized businesses since 1983. While a successful entrepreneur and computer guru, his real passion is personal development. Since 1976 he has committed himself to the study and practice of self-improvement. He is fascinated by the potential that exists within all of us and has sought to understand why some people are successful and fulfilled while others struggle all their lives and never seem to get what they want.

Mark is a Certified Neuro-Associative Conditioning Specialist, achieving his certification from Robbins Research International in 1990. Part of that curriculum taught how to turn fear into power. This included climbing to the top of a 60 foot pole and jumping off while trying to reach a trapeze bar strategically placed out of reach, which he did. He also walked on fire, actually a 30 foot length of hot coals, twice, without getting burned.

Mark's studies over the years include books, audio training and seminars from many well-known names in the field of personal development such as Tony Robbins, Zig Ziglar, Brian Tracy, Bob Proctor, Napoleon Hill, Wayne Dyer, Dale Carnegie, Stephen Covey, Robert Kiyosaki, Deepak Chopra, Jim Rohn, Jack Canfield, Vic Johnson, and many others.

Mark lives in Connecticut with his wife, Lisa, and her dog, Louis.